Techni-Seasonal Commodity Trading

TECHNI-SEASONAL COMMODITY TRADING

By Everet H. Beckner

WINDSOR BOOKS, Brightwaters, New York

Published by Windsor Books
P.O. Box 280
Brightwaters, N.Y., 11718

TABLE OF CONTENTS

ILLUSTRATIONS

Figures

Tables

CHAPTER I

TECHNI-SEASONAL COMMODITY TRADING— An Introduction

I intend to start this book by introducing several of the basic concepts I will be using. The elements of my method consist of: (1) utilizing a *portfolio* approach to *seasonal* trading; (2) implementing *technical* techniques for entry/exit of the trades; and (3) developing and listing the detailed rules and trading results for 30 seasonal trades to be used in the portfolio.

If you had this book in 1971, and had traded the recommended portfolio every year from 1971 through 1982, you would have earned an average return of 375% per year. Your best year (1973) would have shown profits of

828%, while your worst year (1976) would still have shown a 190% return on your money. Since the system is sized and configured to allow you to start any given year with as little as $10,000 in equity, let's assume you started trading with just that amount. An initial investment of $10,000 in 1971 would have made over $640,000 for you during the subsequent 12 years, without reinvesting a single penny of the profits.

If those numbers sound appealing to you, please heed the following advice. I urge you to proceed methodically through the book, and not to look for short-cuts. The seasonal trades described in Chapters VI and VIII are obviously the meatiest and most exciting part of the book, but don't jump ahead. "Financial survival while making consistent profits" is the name of the game in commodity trading, and you must understand and use the material presented in the earlier chapters in order to reach that goal.

The reason to employ a portfolio strategy in any investment program (whether in stocks, bonds, commodities, or even tax shelter partnerships) is to spread your investment dollars across as many potentially profitable trades as possible. This diversification allows you to accommodate the realities of investment events, which inevitably are either better or worse than you expected. By diversifying you can better average out your investment returns. Omnipotent wisdom would allow for a different approach; the real world does not.

Commodity trading is particularly well suited to a portfolio strategy. This is so because you can trade several markets simultaneously with limited funds ($5,000 - $10,000) and during the course of a year can expand the diversification into several other markets. Expanding diversification is possible since most seasonal trades run for only 3-6 months. Not surprisingly, part of the investment strategy is one of developing a portfolio which optimizes this opportunity for diversification without requiring additional capital. The model portfolio which I provide in Chapter VII is constructed in just this way. I selected 18 trades out of a total of 30 described in Chapters VI and VIII, so that no more than 5-7 were active at any one time. This minimizes the equity required to trade the entire portfolio. However, the portfolio still covers 10 different markets, ranging from cotton to pork bellies, and from gold to oats.

The reason for developing seasonal trades for the portfolio has primarily to do with maximizing profits while simultaneously avoiding financial ruin. Furthermore, I believe seasonal trades are inherently the most *reliable* way to trade commodities. I am making this comparison first against "fundamental" trading, which I believe requires too much inside information for the average trader to compete. Similarly, although I own and use a computer for technical analysis, I do not believe a "technical" system can compare with a good seasonal trading system when it comes to reliability and profitability. By technical system, I mean a trading system that is intended generally to be either long or short a particular market (or markets), and which utilizes one or more technical tools(such as moving averages, trend lines, momentum indices, etc.) to signal entry or exit from the long or short positions. My contention that seasonal trades are more reliable and thereby make more money for the average trader is based on the fact that there are many seasonal trades which have been at least 75% reliable for 10-20 years. On the other hand, I don't know of more than two or three technical systems which have been more than 60% reliable in their ratio of winning trades to losing trades over an extended period of time.

If you happen to be in possession of unlimited resources, a trading system which is correct 60% of the time obviously can make you money. However, you do have to be emotionally as well as financially prepared to survive occasional runs of 5 or more losing trades in a row. I use most of Chapter III to elaborate on this road to "financial ruin" and the mathematical laws of probability which must be accomodated if you want to bypass this route. In fact, to avoid "ruin," the single most important element of a trading system is the *reliability* of the trades in the portfolio. **That, for me, says the average trader should develop and use a portfolio of seasonal trades.**

If you, the reader, are also interested in making as much money as possible from your equity—and who isn't—trade "reliability" reenters the picture as the dominant factor. The proof of this statement is once again embedded in the "avoidance of financial ruin" detailed in Chapter III. The only way to make large profits, year after year, relative to the amount of money invested, is to risk as much of your equity as you can prudently afford. This means, simply, that you play the game in such a way that you cannot afford very many losses in a row; otherwise, you will exhaust your capital and have to withdraw from the game. To "stay in the game" you must undertake trades which have established high reliabilities. In order to survive adversity, you must have real confidence in what you are doing and the trades you are taking. Unfortunately, in the real world, it is inevitable that markets sometimes will go against your initial expectations. For any trading system to work it is necessary to avoid panic and premature closing of trades during occasions of temporary adversity. Although computers can handle 5 or 6 losses in a row and continue to trade by the rules contained in the program, most humans realistically cannot. Don't expose yourself to long loss strings if you don't have to. I say again, develop a portfolio of high reliability trades. The best high reliability trades I know of are seasonal trades.

After generally berating technical trading systems, I am now going to tell you that you need to take advantage of technical trading *techniques* in order to develop better seasonal trades. At least, that is what I have done in the trades provided in this book, and they are the best ones I know. The reasons for using technical techniques for seasonal trades have to do entirely with optimizing entry and exit signals for the trades.

Most references on seasonal trades show the "average" behavior of a particular market over the past 10-20 years. Unfortunately, averages are just that. They do not rule out the possibility, for instance, that the Spring up-move in soybeans may start six weeks early (or eight weeks late) this year. You need a way to handle this uncertainty. The rules I have developed for various trades attempt to solve this problem, using such technical tools as trend lines, moving averages, etc. The rules turn out to be different for each trade, because no two markets really trade alike. I developed these rules through long hours spent studying years and years of historical bar charts for the various markets. The rules I provide have been tested for as many years as could reasonably be done (generally 12 years, or more). I know all too well that only "a few years of good trading results do not a reliable system make." This subject, too, is covered more fully in Chapter III.

The common alternative to using technical tools for entry and exit from seasonal trades is to try to pick calendar dates for these actions, and enter and exit each year at these times. Several previous authors have published such seasonal trading books. Unfortunately, the published trading results have inevitably not continued to occur with high reliability in future trades. It is far better, I believe, to do the extra work to develop a better set of entry/exit tools. That really entails applying an assortment of technical methods to get into and out of the trades.

So, what you have in this book is my best effort to pull together all the essential ideas of portfolio theory, seasonal trading strategy, and technical analysis. In addition, I have detailed 30 seasonal trades which, on average, made profits more than 90% of the time from 1971 to 1982. Even in light of this most impressive record, I hope you will read the book carefully and recognize that there are still plenty of ways to lose money in the commodity markets if you don't act with discipline and stick with your plan.

ADVANTAGES OF A PORTFOLIO STRATEGY

Portfolio strategy has evolved as a concept for commodity trading during the past ten years. It's emergence was a natural outgrowth of similar trading strategies employed in the stock market by large mutual and pension fund managers. It is a systematic and sophisticated implementation of the old adage "don't put all your eggs in one basket." In the case of stock market portfolios, such strategies generally result in diversification of the fund into a variety of different investment segments (i.e.—aerospace industries, computers, chemical industries, housing, banking, mining, oil & gas, etc.). The fund managers then attempt to vary with time the relative commitment of funds to the various sub-categories. This is done in such a way as to maximize profits based on their special analytical procedures. In addition to investments in stocks and bonds, of course, fund managers these days also utilize investments in short-term interest bearing instruments as an integral part of their strategies.

The basis of this concept for stock trading is generally attributed to Benjamin Graham (see bibliography). The specific techniques employed today by the many fund managers are so varied, sophisticated, and often esoteric as to be both beyond the scope and unnecessary for the overall purposes of this book. Furthermore, it is not possible to draw a direct connection between portfolio theory as practiced in the stock market and that which might be a logical extension to the commodity market. This is so for several reasons. The principle reason is the relatively fewer number of individual commodities which can be traded as compared with the large number of stocks (a few tens of different commodity markets versus several thousand publicly traded stocks).

Nonetheless, the basic concept of a portfolio strategy can and has been carried over to commodities. Most of the commodity funds in existence today use a fund strategy which consists of: (1) investments in most all of the actively traded markets, and (2) a technical entry/exit technique for trading decisions. In this way, a few commodities which make large moves can result in substantial enough profits to offset the many small losses which accrue from the majority of the markets which "go nowhere" for months at a time. The success (or lack thereof) of such fund portfolios is then most directly connected to the "entry/exit" techniques employed. The arrival and implementation of computer-based trend following systems, derived from 10-30 year data bases of past trading histories, has made all this possible.

This is not to say that there are no "fundamental" trading strategies being employed by commodity fund managers. Rather, that there are fewer fund managers using fundamental strategies than those relying exclusively on technical trading systems. Furthermore, most successful traders will tell you that trying to combine technical and fundamental strategies can often lead to trouble. The two approaches can easily yield opposing recommendations in analyzing whether to be long or short a particular market. Finally, the relative difficulty in obtaining reliable fundamental information on most commodities, and the ease of learning to manipulate data on a computer, combine to produce a dominance of technical portfolio managers in the commodity markets these days. Many of these technical portfolio managers wouldn't recognize a pork belly or a cocoa bean if they saw one.

However, the results of most of the present commodity funds remain relatively unspectacular (in some cases, downright poor). This is because, unlike stock portfolio strategies, few of the present commodity systems operate on other than a purely "technical basis" for their trading decisions. This necessarily results in many, many trades per year, and the attendant large commission costs which must be offset by the relatively few "big winner" trades that come along each year. In 1982, in fact, the 55 registered funds which *Commodities* magazine tracks ended the year with an average loss for all the funds of -1.5%. To be fair, 28 of the funds made profits (the largest being $+37.3\%$). However, 27 registered losses for the year (the worst being -54.1%), and several went belly-up during the year so their record was not entered. Most traders would agree that, in general, 1982 was a particularly difficult year to trade commodities, with many of the markets being flat-to-down most of the year. However, in 1982 my portfolio of seasonal trades returned $+207\%$.

In stock market portfolio strategy, the fundamental values of stocks can play a significant role in buy/sell decisions. Why does this approach not also apply to commodity portfolios? The main reason is that fundamental values for commodities are much more difficult to determine in a timely way. Consider, for example, the problem of determining the size of the corn crop in 1983 and, hence, the probable value of a bushel of corn.

To do this, you first need to know the acreage planted to corn in about 20 states (the U.S. Department of Agriculture tries to supply this data). Then, your concerns shift to the weather conditions during the planting and growing seasons (not only is rainfall important, but so also is temperature). Finally, you have to not only know how many acres of grain actually get harvested but also when they get harvested (late harvests, if the result of bad weather, will reduce the crop due to excessive losses in the field). If you have lived with 10,000 farmers from Illinois to Texas, from March to September, you may know the size of the corn crop better than anyone else in the country. However, at least two things can still go wrong in trying to use this information to make a profitable corn trade: (1) you will be right, but the market will see the situation otherwise and go against you so far that you are stopped out prematurely and have no money with which to trade when the market finally sees it your way; or (2) there will be either a disasterous crop or a bumper crop in soybeans (or wheat) and this competing crop will distort the fundamental value of the corn crop. Again, you were right about the corn crop, but you still lost all your money.

If portfolio strategy is a sound idea, but fundamental approaches are perilous, if not impossible, for the average trader; and technical systems don't make much money; what's a poor trader to do? I'm convinced that the winning approach is the one which I will introduce in this book—the concept of a portfolio of *seasonal* commodity trades. Seasonal trading of commodities has long been recognized as a "higher reliability" way of trading commodities (more winning trades relative to the number of losing trades). However this approach to trading has never been developed to the extent that a sufficient number of good trades in several different markets could be placed together to form a good "seasonal trading portfolio." If done properly, such a portfolio would have a high probability of catching most of the big moves in any given year. At the same time this portfolio would not waste your money on a plethora of worthless, small trades.

I have attempted to develop such a seasonal portfolio with the 18 trades I will present in Chapter VI of this book. In addition, I supply 12 more seasonal trades in Chapter VIII, which the reader can add to his portfolio strategy if adequately capitalized.

An added feature of seasonal trades is that they generally are related to fundamental events in the growing, harvesting, breeding, building, etc. cycles which are characteristic of the specific commodity markets. As such, they are not easily changed, and carry with them a predictability which every trader seeks. This additional advantage which accompanies a seasonal portfolio strategy is the historical basis of confidence in the large number of profitable trades versus the number of loss trades. The 18 trades I have selected for the portfolio in Chapter VI have been profitable more than 90% of the time over the last 12 years. This means you can plan on having to survive fewer consecutive losing trades, and hence can safely keep a larger percentage of your funds in the market at all times. Simply put, this results in a system which should yield very large profits relative to the money available for investment. The portfolio results displayed in

Chapter VII have averaged approximately 375% profits per year for the past 12 years. Who could ask for more than that!

CHAPTER III

The Phenomenal Importance Of High-Reliability Trades— Or, How To Handle The "Probability of Ruin" And Still Make Large Profits

All traders instinctively know the importance of "high-reliability" trades (trades which can be expected to yield profits year after year while suffering few losses). However, for the investor who is trying to make as much money as possible from a finite amount of money, "high-reliability" trades have an importance which is generally not fully appreciated. That is, they are vitally important in handling the statistical realities of trading which Teweles, Harlow and Stone (see bibliography) labeled the "Probability of Ruin." Their Chapter 10, entitled "Money Management," covers the subject more than adequately, and I will only repeat several of their essential concepts, formulae, and results.

For every trader, whether he be conservative or aggressive, the most important thing in his trading plan should be his ability to financially handle the inevitable "unlucky string of bad trades" to which almost all traders are exposed. An "unlucky string of bad trades" can decrease a trader's capital to such an extent that he is unable to stay in the game to participate in the profitable trades which are sure to follow if his trading system is sound. These are simple statistical facts of life for any system that is sound, but necessarily expects a certain percentage of loss trades. This "avoidance of ruin" is a fundamental mathematical concept based on probability theory dating back over 100 years.

One point which is not emphasized by Teweles, et al, and which I believe is crucial to remember, is that probability theory is inherently dependent on the existence of large sample sizes. That is, the trading system must be based on and played out in such a way that a large number of trades are recorded. This allows the expected ratio of profit and loss trades to be statistically realized. We will revisit this point later in this chapter.

There are several concepts and terms which must be defined in order to proceed with this chapter. First, we define the "trading unit." If a trader has $10,000 and is willing to risk $2500 on each trade, he has $10,000/$2,500 = 4 trading units. We will use the letter "C" to denote the number of trading units being considered in our analysis.

Now we must deal with the concept of the "Trader's Advantage." The "Trader's Advantage" is made up of two parts: (1) the mathematical odds of winning versus losing, and (2) the dollars you will win versus the dollars you will lose, depending upon the outcome of the trade. The first part of the concept, the "mathematical advantage," is simply the difference between the probability of winning versus losing. If we use the shorthand notation "%P" and "%L" for the percentage of winning trades or percentage of losing trades to be expected then:

$$\text{Mathematical Advantage} = (\%P - \%L)/100$$

If, for example, odds are 60/40 that a trade will return profits rather than losses, we see the following:

$$\text{Mathematical Advantage} = (60 - 40)/100 = 0.20$$

As we all know, there's more to the game than this. It is important to know the relative value of the profits expected from winning trades versus the value of the losses which accompany losing trades. Simply stated, a few large winning trades can offset a lot of small losing trades, and vice-versa. Using "$P" to stand for the expected value of the winning trades and "$L" to mean the money expected to be lost on the losing trades, the mathematical equation to represent this concept is:

$$\text{Dollar Weighted Mathematical Advantage} = [(\%P)(\$P) - (\%L)(\$L)]/100$$

This term is generally called the "expectation" of the game.

To go one step further, we need an equation which is "normalized" so that the maximum value for the "perfect trade" has the numerical value of one. This is done by a mathematical technique called "normalization" and yields the equation we call the "Trader's Advantage":

$$\text{Trader's Advantage} = \frac{(\%P)(\$P) - (\%L)(\$L)}{(\%P)(\$P) + (\%L)(\$L)}$$

This equation, the "Trader's Advantage," will henceforth be denoted "A" in this book. It will be used as a primary rating tool for evaluation of the relative merit of the trades recommended in Chapters VI and VIII. We must recognize a particular constraint that is associated with this equation. That is, the numerator of the equation must be greater than zero for the equation to be of interest. If the numerator is less than zero, the equation has a negative value, which identifies the trade in question as being a guaranteed losing trade.

So, our primary screening tool for evaluating the recommended seasonal trade is:

$$A = \frac{(\%P)(\$P) - (\%L)(\$L)}{(\%P)(\$P) + (\%L)(\$L)}$$

We see, as desired, that a perfect trade will have %L = 0, and:

$$A = (\%P)\ (\$P)/(\%P)\ (\$P) = 1$$

Furthermore, this equation for ''A'' can be substituted directly into the Tables 10-1, 10-2, and 10-3 in Teweles, et al. There the subject of ''probabilities of ruin'' is treated in exquisite detail for trades where the dollars expected from profitable trades are equal to the dollars from losing trades. The advantage of equation (1) is that it can be used with different values for $P and $L, as well as different values for %P and %L.

Now we can use the Teweles, et al, equation for the ''Probability of Ruin'' in a general way. This equation is derived from standard probability theory, and states the condition for financial survival if you are trading ''C'' trading units, and your trading system possesses a ''Trader's Advantage,'' A:

$$R = [(1 - A)/(1 + A)]^C$$

This is the equation for the ''Probability of Ruin.'' If the value of R for a particular trading plan is near unity, your chances of financial survival approach ZERO. This can occur either because the value of A was too small (low reliability trade), or because the value of C was too small (too much of your equity at risk on a single trade), or both. So, our task is to find an optimum balance between a good system with a large ''A,'' and a reasonably conservative trading strategy that will make ''C'' large enough for survival. This will allow us to invest a substantial portion of our equity and thereby make large profits.

We need to go through a few examples to illustrate the power of the equation for the probability of ruin, R. First, let's be conservative in our approach to money commitment. We'll retain 75% of our funds in reserve, but use a system which on average has only 55% profitable trades and for which the average profit is 30% greater than the money lost in the losing trades. If we plan to commit 25% of our money, then C = 4. Here we first obtain A and then calculate the probability of ruin:

$$A = [(\%P)(\$P) - (\%L)(\$L)]/[(\%P)(\$P) + (\%L)(\$L)]$$
$$= [(.55)(1.3) - (.45)(1.0)]/[(.55)(1.3) + (.45)(1.0)]$$
$$= [.265]/[1.65] = 0.23$$

Then, $R = [(1-A)/(1+A)]^C$
$$= [(1-0.23)/(1+0.23)]^4$$
$$= [0.63]^4 = 0.16$$

This says that our "conservative" trader has a 16% chance of being wiped-out by a bad string of losing trades, in spite of initially investing only 25% of his money in the market.

Now, let's look at a so-called "risky" approach. Here we invest 50% of our capital in each trade, but utilize a "high-reliability" system which produces 80% winning trades. As before, we will assume that the profitable trades make 30% more than is lost on the losing trades. For this case, C = 2. Again, we obtain A:

$$A = [(.80)(1.3) - (.20)(1.0)]/[(.80)(1.3) + (.20)(1.0)]$$
$$= [.84]/[1.24] = 0.68$$

Then, $R = [(1-A)/(1+A)]^C$
$$= [(1-.68)/(1+.68)]^2$$
$$= [0.19]^2 = 0.036$$

Behold, our probability of ruin is only 3.6%, for an initial strategy which appeared to be quite risky.

These two examples illustrate fully, I believe, the overwhelming importance of developing a trading system which yields a much larger number of winning trades than losing trades. I contend that the best possibility of developing such a system is through observation of seasonal tendencies in markets over many years of trading. I will attempt to illustrate such a system in Chapters VI and VIII, using 30 seasonal trades I have developed from testing back data over the past 12 years. The average "Trader's Advantage" for all the trades is in excess of 0.93. This means the probability of ruin is very, very low. If you think there must be some catch to

23

this story—there may be! There is an unavoidable weakness in the fact that the "sample size," which I mentioned earlier, is relatively small. However, this should pose no problem as explained below.

For any given trade in the system, we are dealing with only 12 years of history (12 trades). In most cases, fewer than 2 of those trades were losses. Reverting again to statistical probabilities, and using Table 10-1 of Teweles, et al, (see below) we observe the following. Take the case of a rather mediocre trade having a value for A of only 10%, but with only 10 trades having been observed. We see from the Table (line 2), that there is only a 49.6% probability of observing more than 4 losing trades out of the first 10, although we expect to always observe exactly 45% of the trades as losses. In fact, further inspection of the Table shows that there is a 10% probability of observing fewer than two losing trades out of the first 10 (suggesting an 80% reliable trade although we know it is only 55% reliable). If we go further with this exercise, however, and extend our observations to 20 trades, the possibility of observing such an unexpectedly favorable result from our system diminishes to only 2%. We see from this example that the larger the number of trades observed, the better (50-100 trades are clearly an adequate sample). However, if approached with some caution, 10-15 years of trading history is a reasonable situation to work with. We must simply bear in mind that we are working with "statistically limited" trading results and that past performance does not guarantee future performance.

TABLE 10-1 PROBABILITY OR MORE THAN p PERCENT UNSUCCESSFUL TRADES WITH A PROBABILITY .55 OF WINNING (10 PERCENT ADVANTAGE)*

No. of trades	P→ 0	10	20	30	40	50	60	70	80	90	100
5	.9497		.7438		.4069		.1312		.0185		.0000
10	.9975	.9767	.9004	.7340	.4956	.2616	.1020	.0274	.0045	.0003	.0000
20	1.0000	.9991	.9811	.8701	.5857	.2493	.0580	.0064	.0003	.0000	.0000
30	1.0000	1.0000	.9960	.9306	.6408	.2309	.0334	.0016	.0000	.0000	.0000
40	1.0000	1.0000	.9993	.9717	.7376	.2624	.0283	.0007	.0000	.0000	.0000
50	1.0000	1.0000	.9998	.9835	.7615	.2385	.0165	.0002	.0000	.0000	.0000
60	1.0000	1.0000	.9999	.9903	.7820	.2180	.0097	.0001	.0000	.0000	.0000
70	1.0000	1.0000	1.0000	.9942	.7998	.2002	.0058	.0000	.0000	.0000	.0000
80	1.0000	1.0000	1.0000	.9965	.8156	.1844	.0035	.0000	.0000	.0000	.0000
90	1.0000	1.0000	1.0000	.9979	.8294	.1706	.0021	.0000	.0000	.0000	.0000
100	1.0000	1.0000	1.0000	.9987	.8426	.1574	.0013	.0000	.0000	.0000	.0000
150	1.0000	1.0000	1.0000	.9999	.8909	.1091	.0001	.0000	.0000	.0000	.0000
200	1.0000	1.0000	1.0000	1.0000	.9209	.0791	.0000	.0000	.0000	.0000	.0000
250	1.0000	1.0000	1.0000	1.0000	.9440	.0560	.0000	.0000	.0000	.0000	.0000
300	1.0000	1.0000	1.0000	1.0000	.9592	.0408	.0000	.0000	.0000	.0000	.0000
400	1.0000	1.0000	1.0000	1.0000	.9778	.0222	.0000	.0000	.0000	.0000	.0000
500	1.0000	1.0000	1.0000	1.0000	.9877	.0123	.0000	.0000	.0000	.0000	.0000

Table taken from *"The Commodity Futures Game"*
By R.J.Teweles, C.V.Harlow & H.L.Stone

Another way of saying all this is that, although I am presenting a system containing 350 trades dating back over 12 years with more than 90% of the trades being profitable, don't mortgage the house to trade it. Though it looks like a certain winner and I'm sure it would have been a terrific system to trade from 1971 to 1982, the sample size is still too small to ignore certain fundamental aspects of probability theory. I only know the trades have worked very well in the past, and believe that seasonal commodity trades have an extra validity which derives from their association with the fundamental seasonal factors of those markets. If those factors continue to hold true in the future, then I am providing you with a system which should yield profits near 400% per year.

CHAPTER IV

SEASONAL TRADING CONCEPTS AND HISTORICAL DATA

Seasonal price patterns of many commodities have been recognized for many years, and several previous authors have advocated incorporating these tendencies into trading systems. However, before we venture very far into this subject, I think we should lay a little groundwork regarding what we really mean by seasonal patterns and the way they can be used in a commodity trading program. First, the reader should be aware that there are both "cash" seasonal patterns and "futures" seasonal patterns. The cash seasonal patterns are those established by the cash markets for commodities. These seasonal patterns have been followed for many years. Such patterns are dominated by certain events that necessarily occur year after year in the production or utilization of that particular commodity. An example would be the seasonal weakness in wheat which tends to commence in February and extend into July when the harvest is underway. Consequently, cash seasonal charts contain trends that can be considered the crop size is pretty well determined by then. One of the best modern treatments of cash seasonal trends is contained in Dr. Bruce Gould's book, *"Commodity Trading Manual"* (see bibliography). The most important feature of cash seasonals, compared to futures seasonals, is the fact that there are literally decades of data available to be compiled and analyzed. Subsequently, cash seasonal charts contain trends that can be considered statistically significant. The weakness of cash seasonal patterns, and it is a serious one for anyone who is trying to use them for guidance in trading the futures markets, is that futures markets often diverge significantly from cash prices. An easy way to illustrate this is to look at some seasonal charts for cash markets and compare them with seasonal charts for the corresponding futures markets.

The most recent and comprehensive book devoted exclusively to commodity seasonal chart patterns is the one by Grushcow and Smith (see bibliography). I have provided a reproduction in Figure 1 of their charts for cash hogs and for December Hog futures. In Figure 2, I show similar data for cash soybeans and for January Soybean futures. These charts, and others from the book by Grushcow and Smith, and still others from Bernstein, will be used throughout this book. The format of the charts needs some explanation for those of you who are unfamiliar with it. The original charts from Grushcow and Smith actually contain more information than I have reproduced here; however, we need only seasonal trends for the present book, and that is precisely what is contained in the figures. You see in Figure 2 that the seasonal trend for cash soybeans is "up" from January till June, based on the past 24 years of data, and then "down" from early June till October. (Remember, these are "average data" for the past 24 years of trading, and cannot be expected to be followed exactly every year. Additional information on the "reliability" of these trends is contained in Grushcow and Smith). To further illustrate the charts, you see in Figure 2 that the seasonal trend for January Soybean futures does not commence its upward move until late April-early May, based on 11 years of futures data, and generally peaks-out by August. I believe the case is clear from these two figures that, although the data is more plentiful and reliable for cash commodity markets, we must concentrate on futures market data as we develop our strategies and our trades for seasonal trading of the commodity markets.

To my knowledge, the first extensive compilation and publication of seasonal patterns for *futures* markets was done by J. Bernstein in 1979 (see bibliography). Due to that work of Bernstein, and more recently to the more comprehensive work of Grushcow and Smith, a ten to twenty year data base is now available for use in developing specific seasonal trades based on their established seasonal price patterns. We have the computer revolution to thank for this, since computers have made it relatively easy to compile and analyze data. They have been immensely helpful in developing the price trends and pattern reliabilities for the multitude of markets currently being traded.

FIGURE 1

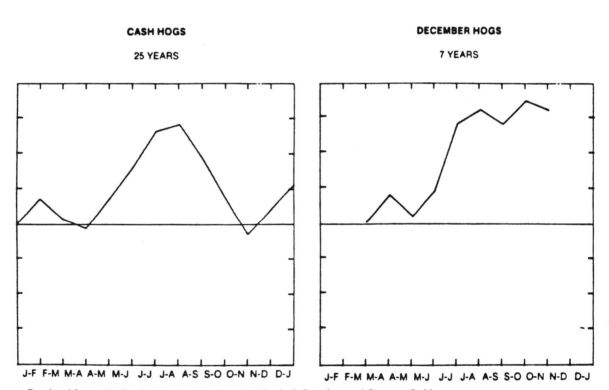

Reprinted from "Profits Through Seasonal Trading" by Jack Gruschow and Courtney Smith
Courtesy of J. Wiley and Sons, publisher

29

FIGURE 2

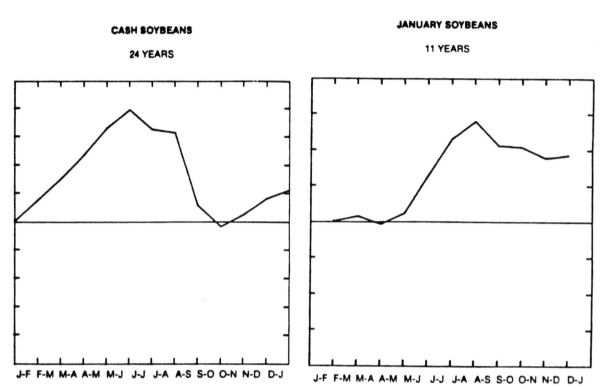

Reprinted from *"Profits Through Seasonal Trading"* by Jack Gruschow and Courtney Smith
Courtesy of J. Wiley and Sons, publisher.

This is the starting point I have used to develop the trades in this book. It is, however, only the starting point, because specific entry/exit techniques still have to be developed for each trade. In fact, this latter task is much more difficult than merely obtaining and understanding the "average" seasonal pattern for a particular commodity. To develop the detailed trade rules for the material contained in Chapters VI and VIII, I have gone over every year of historical bar chart data available, on a day-by-day basis, to ascertain that the entry/exit rules really work. It is easy, for example, to observe from the charts of Grushcow and Smith that, on average, December Cocoa goes up in price from May into December. It's quite another matter to develop a specific set of entry and exit rules that returns substantial profits for 11 out of the 12 years from 1971 to 1982. I have done this necessary analysis and developed the trading rules for the 30 different trades in Chapter VI and VIII.

Several earlier books have attempted to provide a collection of seasonal trading recommendations, most recently Williams and Noseworthy (see bibliography). However, none of these earlier systems have continued to yield the profitable trades which appeared to be there when the books were published. This failure has resulted, I believe, from the simplistic entry/exit rules recommended for the trades, rather than from significant changes in seasonal patterns for the trades. For instance, most of the previous trade recommendations contained little more than "specific dates" for entry and exit from the trades. We now know that such a simplistic approach does not provide seasonal trades that stand the test of time. I have rectified this problem, I believe, by using several basic technical trading tools for entry/exit signals in the trades outlined in Chapters VI and VIII.

Of the 30 trades contained in Chapters VI and VIII, some have stronger and more extensive seasonal data backing them up than others. This supporting seasonal data can take either of two forms: (1) there is a strong, obvious correlation between the direction of the specific trade and the features of the seasonal chart; or (2) there is a less strong correlation between the trade direction and the seasonal data, but in fact the trade data extend over many years with high reliability. This will become more obvious as we go through the material in Chapters VI and VIII on a trade-by-trade basis.

CHAPTER V

ENTRY/EXIT TECHNIQUES USED IN THE TRADES

There are several entry/exit techniques which I have developed for use in the trades detailed in Chapters VI and VIII. You will note as you go through those chapters that each trade does have its own individual set of trading rules, but that also all the trades utilize the technical tools outlined in this chapter for entry, exit, or reversing a position. The tools are all relatively simple technical techniques, utilizing such things as the breaking of trend lines after a certain calendar date, season hi's/season lo's, etc. I will list the techniques in this chapter and provide examples of each so that they will be fully understood. Please realize that if you do not understand these techniques, the trades cannot be expected to work for you the way they work for me. In addition, if you are careless, or unable to follow the markets on a daily basis, you're going to get into trouble with the trades.

Most of the trading signals are based on the *closing price* confirming the signal—with entries or exits then made on a "close only" basis. This means that you follow the signal if the market *closes* in such a way that the signal for entry or exit is clearly given. If limit-up or limit-down moves occur on the day the signal is given, then entry or exit from the trade should be made as soon as possible on a subsequent day.

I don't intend to provide a tutorial on the fundamentals of technical trading techniques. For that I recommend the books by Kaufman, by Teweles, et al, and by Sklarew (see bibliography). I will, however, spend a few pages on the specific concepts used for entry and exit signals in the trades described in Chapters VI and VIII.

ENTRY/EXIT SIGNALS

1. *"Trend Line" Signals*

Trade signals originating from the breaking of trendlines are used frequently. They are generally constrained to be used only after a certain calendar date, so as not to get into a trade until the expected seasonal move is underway. In addition, I always specify that the "broken" trendline which is being used to signal entry be of some minimum time duration (such as 4 weeks, 5 weeks, etc.). In fact, a few examples here would probably be more valuable than words. I have displayed a chart in Figure 3 of September 1982 Wheat (reprinted with permission from the chart service of Commodity Perspective, Chicago, Ill.). This chart shows a 17 week trendline being broken on March 22 by the close at 392 for this contract. Similarly, the breaking of a 6-week trendline in July 1982 Corn is shown in Figure 4.

The crucial understanding required for future use of this technique by the reader is that: **(1) the trendline in question must be well established; and (2) time is measured from the most distant intersection of the trendline with the hi (low) of the daily bar chart. Furthermore, if the rules state that breaking of a 6-week trendline is required for entry, obviously a 7-week or 8-week trendline will also qualify, if that is what happens.** However, breaking of a trendline with a shorter duration (say, for example, a 5-week

34

FIGURE 3

35

FIGURE 4

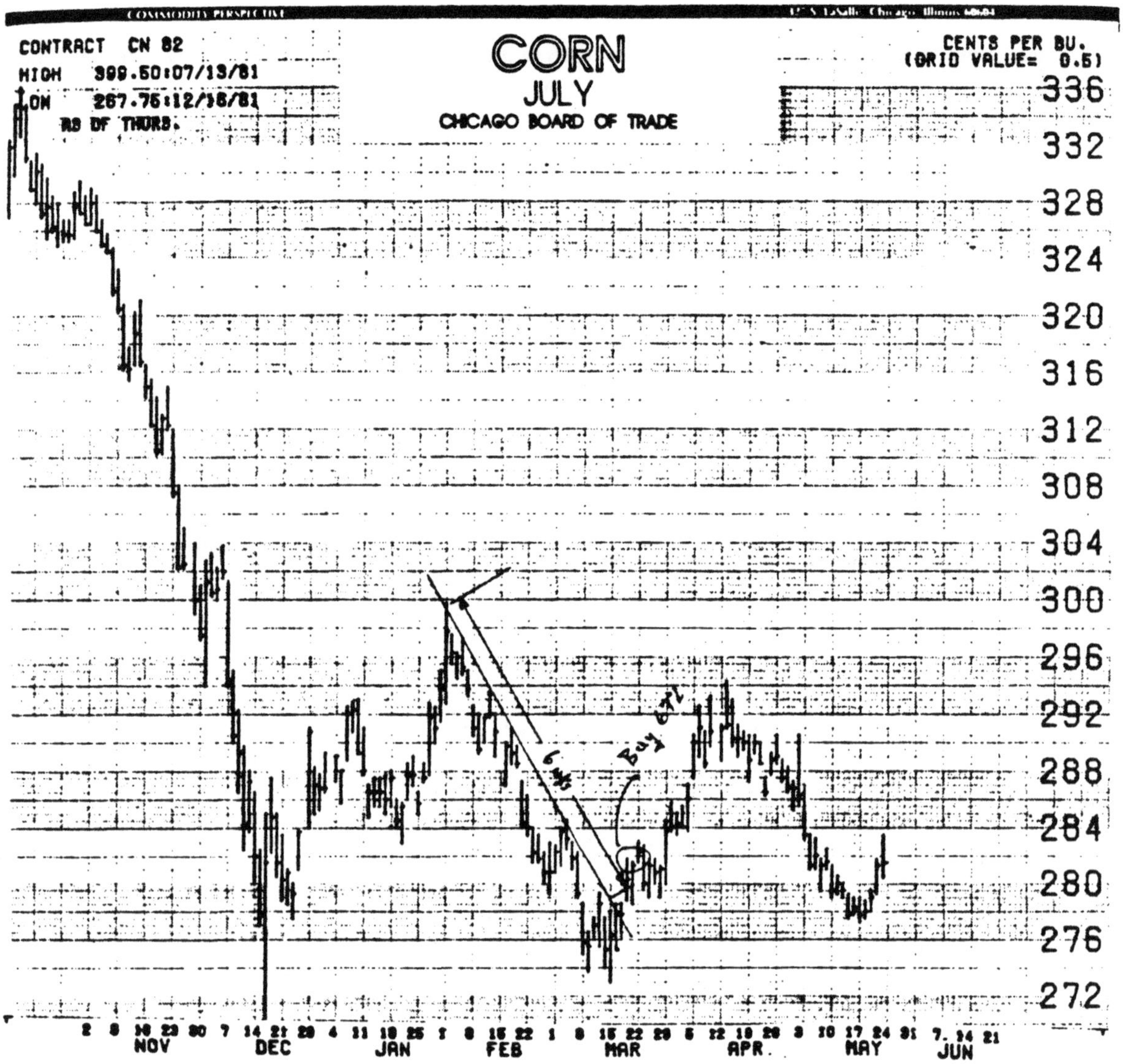
COMMODITY PERSPECTIVE
CONTRACT CN 82
HIGH
LOW
AS OF THURS.
CORN
JULY
CHICAGO BOARD OF TRADE
CENTS PER BU.
(GRID VALUE= 0.5)
336
332
328
324
320
316
312
308
304
300
296
292
288
284
280
276
272
NOV
DEC
JAN
FEB
MAR
APR.
MAY
JUN

+ 4-day trendline) will *not* qualify for this case which specifies a 6-week trendline.

An example of an "unacceptably established" trendline is shown in Figure 5, running from February 16 to March 25 in the June 1982 T-Bill chart. The trendline in question is not "well established" because the market during the week of March 22 did not trade higher than its performance during the week of March 1. By way of contrast, the trendline running from March 30 to May 22 in this chart is already well established as a good 7-week trendline, and is just waiting to be broken by a close below the line.

2. *"Donchian" Signals*

This set of signals is based on ideas attributed to Richard Donchian. Dennis Dunn has also published several articles on this technique, most recently in the June 1982 issue of *"Commodities"* magazine.

The idea of this set of signals is to buy (or sell) when the market closes over (under) the range of trading for the prior *n* weeks (*n* may be 3, 4, 5, etc.). That's all there is to it. One thing to keep in mind is that a "week" consists of those trading days beginning on a Monday and ending on a Friday. In other words, 20 trading days beginning on Wednesday and ending on Tuesday (20 days later) do not constitute "4 weeks" of trading as required by this rule. To qualify, you must be able to start counting on a Monday to determine the number of weeks in the interval under consideration. This may not be the way Donchian or Dunn use the technique, but it's the way I have used it in developing my trades.

Two good examples of the breaking of a 5-week Donchian line for a buy signal, and a 4-week Donchian line for a sell signal, are shown in the March 1982 T-Bill chart in Figure 6.

3. *"Season High or Season Low" Signals*

This is a signal to enter or exit a trade whenever prices close higher than the contract season high, or lower than the contract season low. Obviously, this is a special case of the Donchian signal just described above. An example of a season high entry signal is shown in Figure 7 in the December 1982 Heating Oil chart. In this case, you would not buy on May 7 with the close at 9480, since the close is not above the season high. Rather, you would wait for the close on May 10 at 9580.

37

FIGURE 5

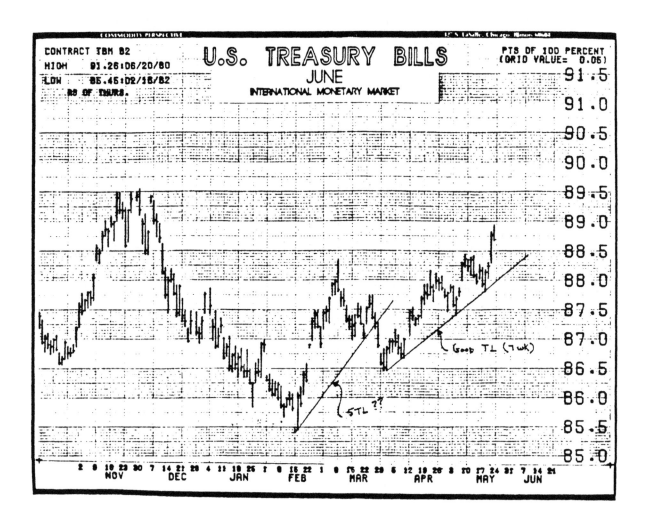

FIGURE 6

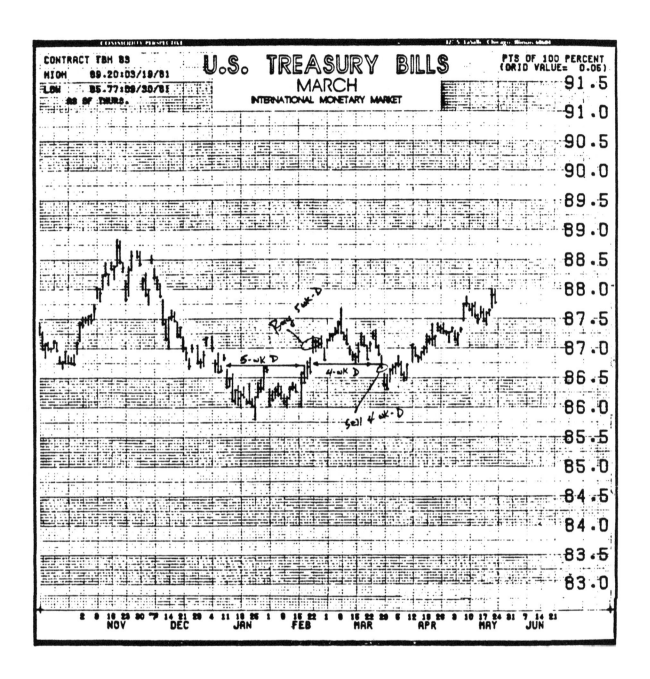

FIGURE 7

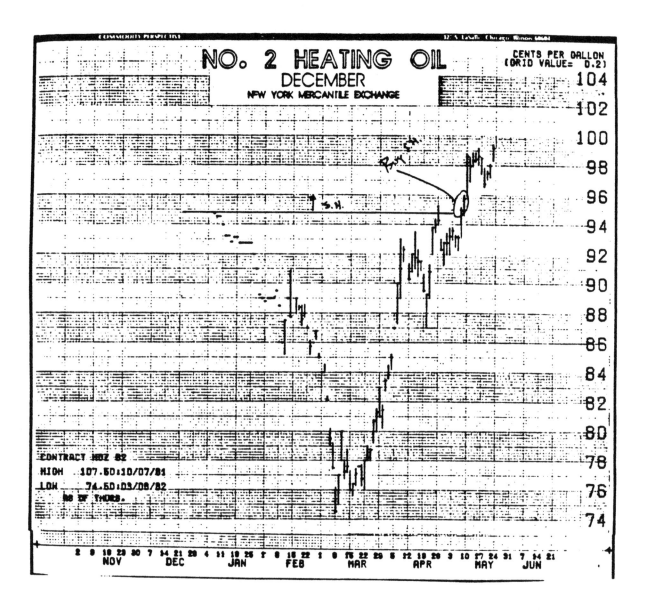

4. *"Higher (Lower) Close Than Prior Three Days" Signals*

This signal is always used in connection with some specific calendar date or with some profit level being achieved in a trade. For a buy signal, it specifies that you enter long (or sometimes is used to close a short trade) when the market closes *higher* than any of the closes for the prior 3 trading days. Similarly, for a sell signal, you would enter short (or close a long position, if open) on this signal when the market closed *lower* than any of the prior three trading days' closing prices. The shorthand notation that I use for this trade signal is 1HC3 for action on the 1st close higher than the prior three days' closes. For action on the 1st close lower than the close of the prior three days, I use 1LC3. An example of a 1HC3 entry is shown in the chart for June 1982 Eurodollars in Figure 8.

For a few of the trades, "trading range" is substituted for "closing price" for the prior three days being considered for this signal.

SUMMARY

To summarize, the trade signals used are:

1. 4TL, 5TL, etc.:	The signal occurs when the market closes over or under a trend line drawn across several daily market highs or lows dating back in time 4-weeks, 5-weeks, etc.
2. 4wk-D, 5wk-D, etc.:	D refers to a trading technique credited to R. Donchian, which requires that the market *close* higher (lower) than the prior full 4-weeks or full 5-weeks, etc. of the trading range to buy (sell).
3. S.H. or S.L.:	This is a signal to enter or exit a trade whenever prices close higher than the contract season high, or lower than the contract season low.
4. 1HC3 or 1LC3:	1HC3 is my shorthand for a signal to enter or exit the trade as soon as there is a close *higher* than the close on the prior three days of trading; similarly, 1LC3 specifies trade action on a close *lower* than the close on the three prior days of trading.

ADDITIONAL DEFINITIONS

Before completing this chapter, I need to define a few more trade signal

41

FIGURE 8

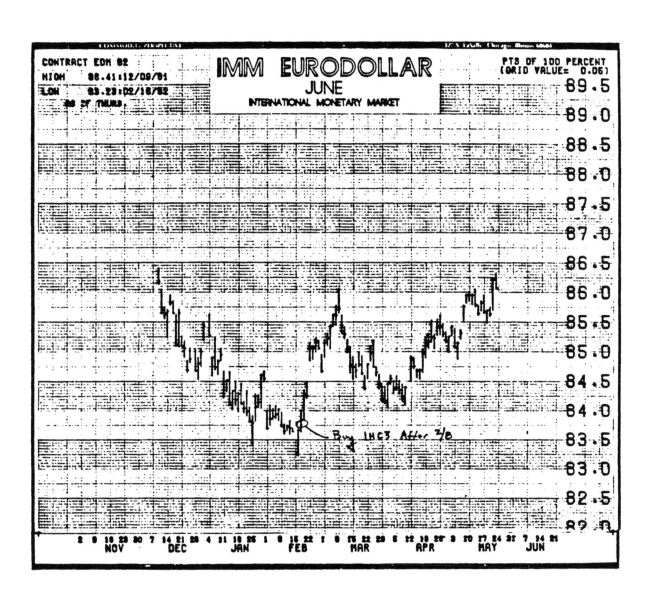

concepts used in Chapters VI and VIII.

1. Lest there be any doubt, all trades are signaled using daily bar charts for the appropriate contract.

2. "Reverse Stop": This is a protective stop signal which requires that a position be *reversed* from either "long" to "short," or from "short" to "long" if the stop is signaled. So, for instance, if the trade position was *long* one contract of November beans (SX), then a "reverse stop" signal would require that you sell two contracts of SX—one to close out the long position and one to go short 1 contract of SX.

3. "Double Reverse Stop": This is a protective stop signal like the "reverse stop" signal in (2), except that you DOUBLE THE SIZE OF THE TRADE POSITION if the signal is given. For instance, if you were long one contract of February bellies (PBG) and the double reverse stop signal was given, then you would sell *three* contracts of PBG—one contract to close out the long PBG position, and two contracts to go short double the number of contracts you were originally long.

4. " 4% Profit, *10%* Profit, etc.": This is a technique employed to determine positions for stops and/or to determine prices at which to close-out trades and take profits. For example, a *10%* profit in a trade would mean that prices changed by 10% from the entry price for that trade. So , if the trade instruction is to "take 10% profits," and you are long December corn (CZ) at a price of $3.00/bu., then you should take profits when CZ reaches $3.30/bu. [$3.00 plus 0.10 ($3.00) = $3.30]. Similarly, a 4% loss stop on this $3.00 long CZ position would be located at $2.88 [$3.00 minus 0.04 ($3.00) = $3.00 − $0.12 = $2.88].

5. "Short Trade Equivalent": This is a trade instruction used occasionally for trades which are generally *long* trades and for which a set of rules is provided for entry and exit from such *long* trades. However, occasionally the trade is reversed to a *short* position, and the instruction is given to use the "short trade equivalent" of several of the previously stated rules. It means that if, for instance, the previous rule for the long trade was "*sell* stop located at *S.L.* close," the "short trade equivalent" of that rule would be "*buy* stop located at *S.H.* close."

Two last reminders are in order regarding the chart format to use for following the various trades and determining signals. (a) You should maintain a daily bar chart for the contract month specified in the trade rules, showing the high, low, and close for each day. (b) Do not try to trade from a "nearby contract" chart. For instance, do not try to trade February bellies from a March belly chart. Sometimes you find you don't have a good chart for the trade specified, and you will be tempted to use a substitute chart from another nearby month of the commodity. I assure you, sometimes that will work, but sometimes it won't! The rules I have provided and the trade results are all based on trading from the daily bar chart for the specified month of the commodity, and no other month.

CHAPTER VI

THE 18 SEASONAL TRADES FOR THE MODEL PORTFOLIO

This chapter contains the details of 18 seasonal trades incorporated in the portfolio analysis of Chapter VII. Each trade is treated separately, with its own set of entry/exit/reverse rules and documented trade results for the years 1971-1982. The only exception to this time period is for two seasonal trades in gold. These trades run only from 1975 to 1982 since the gold market did not trade until 1975 on a futures exchange. The trade results listed for each trade are as accurate as possible, although I cannot guarantee that there are absolutely no errors. I have done all the analysis and checked them thoroughly so the possibility of error is slight.

I have included with each trade (except the gold trades) the applicable seasonal charts for the particular commodity. These charts have been reprinted with permission from the book by Grushcow and Smith, or the book by Bernstein (for the spread trades). I have added a heavily shaded line to the original charts which, for each case, indicates the specific time period during which the trade is applicable, as well as the normal direction of the seasonal trade. For further information on the format and content in these figures, look back to Chapter IV and the text associated with Figure 2.

I have limited the trades in the portfolio to 18, and have intentionally spaced the timing of the trades out over the year. By spacing out the trades, it is now very possible to trade the entire portfolio on $10,000 initial equity and generally not have more than 50% of the account funds committed. In fact, the maximum amount ever required was in 1976, when $23,000 investment equity was necessary in order to maintain the 50% safety factor. This strategy was discussed extensively in Chapter III. There I tried to prove that such a strategy was acceptably conservative in terms of financial survival, yet still provided the desired high return on equity. In fact, the portfolio results displayed in Chapter VII demonstrate the latter point convincingly. To give you a better view of the trade distribution across the calendar year, I have produced Figure 9 to give you a visual presentation of the portfolio trade actions anticipated each year.

The trades outlined in this chapter are numbered from 1 to 18, according to the time of the year when they are normally entered. From Figure 9, you can see we begin with trades entered in December. Table 1 lists all the trades (identified by their abbreviations), their approximate entry dates, % of profitable years, Trader's Advantage (A), and Rank Order based on the relative value of "A."

We see from this table that an additional screening criteria is required to handle the fact that several trades have the same value for the Trader's Advantage, A. For evaluating the rank order of many trades, I recommend using the "average profits divided by margin required" as a secondary screening factor. This additional term has been evaluated for each trade

FIGURE 9

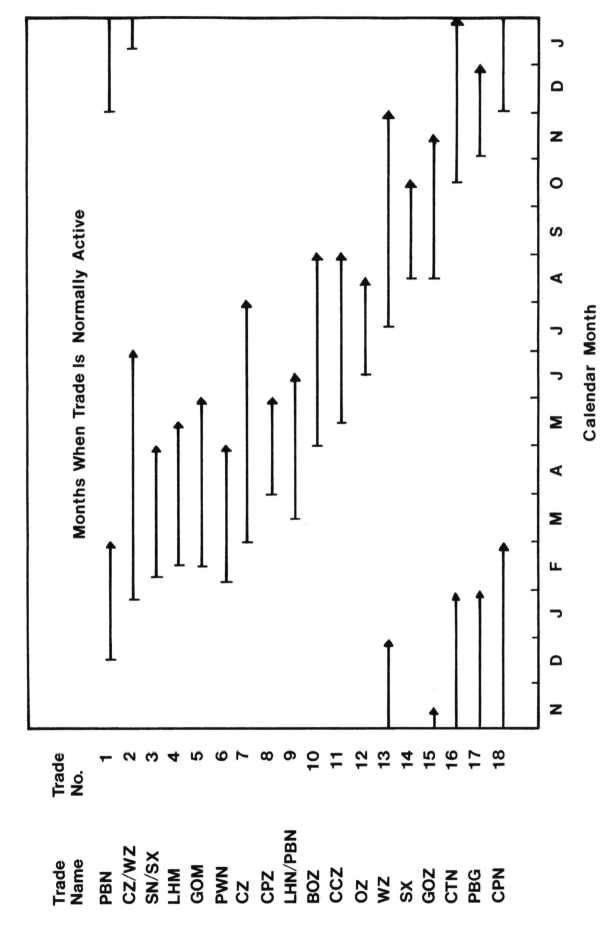

TABLE 1

Trade #	Trade	App'x. Entry Date	% Profit Yrs.	"A"	Rank Order Based on "A"
1	PBN	12/15	100%	1.0	1
2	CZ/WZ	1/15	75%	0.94	5
3	SN/SX	2/1	100%	1.0	1
4	LHM	2/1	100%	1.0	1
5	GOM	2/1	100%	1.0	1
6	PWN	2/7	100%	1.0	1
7	CZ	3/1	75%	0.84	10
8	CPZ	3/15	89%	0.95	3
9	LHN/PBN	3/1	90%	0.87	9
10	BOZ	5/1	92%	0.95	3
11	CCZ	5/1	92%	0.92	7
12	OZ	6/1	83%	0.93	6
13	WZ	7/1	100%	1.0	1
14	SX	8/4	100%	1.0	1
15	GOZ	8/15	100%	1.0	1
16	CTN	10/1	100%	1.0	1
17	PBG	11/1	92%	0.98	2
18	CPN	11/15	91%	0.90	8
		Average:	93%	0.96	

and appears in Table 2 where I arrive at the final rank order for all the trades in the portfolio. Table 2 also contains a column showing the number of profit years, loss years, and "no trade" years for each trade (column P/L/N.T.). I have presented Tables 1 and 2 mainly to provide a framework for the reader to judge the relative merits of the several trades in this book, and as a means of evaluating any other trades he wishes to compare with these. The reader can use these data, for instance, to add or substitute trades into the model portfolio if he so desires.

TABLE 2

†Rank Order	Trade	Trade #	"A"	*Avg. Profit/ Marg. Req'd.	P/L/N.T.
1	SN/SX	3	1.0	6.06	6/0/6
2	WZ	13	1.0	3.67	7/0/5
3	LHM	4	1.0	1.97	9/0/3
4	SX	14	1.0	1.50	10/0/2
5	PWN	6	1.0	1.35	11/0/1
6	GOZ	15	1.0	1.33	8/0/0
7	CTN	16	1.0	1.29	12/0/0
8	PBN	1	1.0	1.05	12/0/0
9	GOM	5	1.0	0.58	8/0/0
10	PBG	17	0.98	1.22	11/1/0
11	BOZ	10	0.95	2.16	11/1/0
12	CPZ	8	0.95	0.93	8/1/3
13	CZ/WZ	2	0.94	1.92	9/3/0
14	OZ	12	0.93	1.82	10/2/0
15	CCZ	11	0.92	1.52	11/1/0
16	CPN	18	0.90	1.56	10/1/1
17	CZ	7	0.85	3.11	9/3/0
18	LHN/PBN	9	0.85	1.08	9/1/2
		Average:	0.96	1.90	

† Rank Order is based first on the value for "A," and second on the value for "Average Profit/Margin Required."

* "Average Profit/Margin Required" is based on approximate current prices and margin costs.

The remainder of this chapter is devoted to listing the trading rules and results for the 18 trades recommended for the model portfolio. A few sentences are provided for each trade to give you insight into the basis for the trade strategy for that particular trade.

Following the summary and the trade rules for each trade, I have supplied the year-by-year details of all the trade entries and exits, including the particular rule that was used for each entry/exit. In order to take into account the price differences that have occurred over the past 12 years (hogs have ranged in price from $20.00 to $60.00 per ctw, for example), profits and losses were first computed on a "percent of entry price" basis, and then converted to dollars of profit or loss based on 1982 nominal prices. The right hand column of each table contains this profit/loss information. In addition, at the head of the column, the 1982 average price on which the particular commodity is based is pointed out.

Trade #1
JULY PORK BELLIES (PBN)

This trade is designed to catch the seasonal up-move which normally occurs in July Pork Bellies in December-March. To date, it has been entered long 11 out of 12 years since 1971, with 3 of the 11 long trades subsequently being reversed to short. It has thereby been profitable 100% of the years since 1971, with an average profit of $2100 per contract per year (based on 65¢ bellies). Based on a value for the "Trader's Advantage" of A = 1.0, and the value for Avg. Profits/Margin Req'd. of 1.05, it ranks 8th in value out of the 18 trades in the portfolio.

HISTORICAL RECORD:

1. Total Years Observed: 12
      Profit Years: 12
      Loss Years: 0
      No Trade Years: 0
2. %Profitable Years: 100%
3. % Loss Years: 0
4. Average Profit/Year: $2104 (basis $65.00 PBN)
5. Average Loss/Year: $ 0
6. **Trader's Advantage: 1.0**
7. (Average Annual Trade Profits)/Margin Required: 1.05

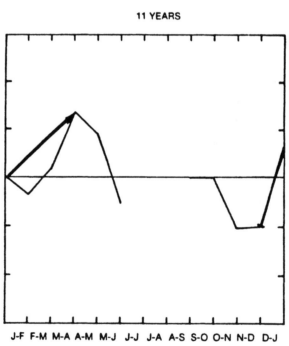

JULY PORK BELLIES

11 YEARS

J-F F-M M-A A-M M-J J-J J-A A-S S-O O-N N-D D-J

Reprinted from *'''Profits Through Seasonal Trading''* by Jack Gruschow and Courtney Smith
Courtesy of J. Wiley and Sons, publisher.

Rules For Trade #1
JULY PORK BELLIES (PBN)

Generally, the trade is first entered as a *long* trade, and the rules are as follows:

1. After 12/15, buy long July Pork Bellies on the first close which is at least 25 points higher than the *range* of the prior 3 days of trading.

2. After entry, protect the position with a stop (close only) on an 8 wk-D signal. Continue to update the location of this stop on a weekly basis. If stopped out at a loss, sell the long position and also go short *two* contracts for each original long contract. Hold these two contracts for a profit equal to: 100 points each; or, a combined profit equal to 2-times the original loss, whichever is greater. When achieved, close the trade.

3. If no entry via rules (1) or (5) has been made by the end of December, buy PBN on the close on 12/31 (or the last trading day in December).

4. Hold entries made by rules (1), (3), or (5) for a profit equal to 9% of the entry price. When reached, close the position on the first close which is lower than any of the closes of the prior 3 days of trading. Continue to update the location of this closing instruction on a daily basis until the trade is closed.

Occasionally, the trade should first be entered as a short PBN trade. The rules for this case are:

5. After 12/25, sell short PBN on any season low (S.L) close. If done, trade this short position and close it via the "short trade equivalent" of rules (2) and (4). See Chapter IV for "short trade equivalent" instructions.

6. Enter long PBN via (1) - (3), or short via (5), whichever occurs first. Do not enter both ways.

Historical Results For Trade # 1
JULY PORK BELLIES (PBN)

Margin: $2000

CY*	ENTRY DATE	RULE #	L/S	PRICE	EXIT DATE	RULE #	PRICE	P/L (points)	P/L (%)	$ P/L (basis $65.00 PBN)
1971	12/28/70	5	S	27.50	1/19/71	4	25.00	+ 250	+ 9.1	+ 2170
1972	12/17/71	1	L	34.75	1/19/72	4	38.80	+ 405	+ 11.7	+ 2800
1973	12/31/72	3	L	46.00	3/16/73	4	55.00	+ 900	+ 19.6	+ 4750
1974	12/27/73	1	L	61.00	1/19/74	4	64.00	+ 300	+ 4.9	+ 1135
1975	12/31/74	3	L	63.80	2/ 7/75	2	67.60	+ 380	+ 6.0	+ 1390
1976	12/22/75	1 or 3	L	70.70	4/14/76	4	76.00	+ 530	+ 7.5	+ 1775
1977	12/16/76	1	L	52.65	1/ 6/77	4	56.00	+ 335	+ 6.4	+ 1490
1978	12/16/77	1	L	51.10	1/12/78	4	58.30	+ 720	+ 14.1	+ 3410
1979	12/18/78	1	L	63.00	12/19/78	2	60.00	- 300 } + 460	+ 7.3	+ 1580
	12/19/78	2	S(2)	60.00	12/26/78	2	56.20	+ 760 }		
1980	12/31/79	3	L	50.90	1/ 8/80	2	48.00	- 290 } + 290	+ 5.7	+ 1180
	1/ 8/80	2	S(2)	48.90	1/14/80	2	46.90	+ 580 }		
1981	12/19/80	1	L	69.50	1/ 2/81	2	60.60	- 890 } + 890	+ 12.8	+ 2940
	1/ 2/81	2	S(2)	60.60	3/ 4/81	2	57.70	+1780 }		
1982	12/17/81	1	L	58.00	1/11/82	4	63.70	+ 570	+ 9.8	+ 2350

* CY = Calendar Year

All P/L Results Include Commission Costs

52

Trade #2
DECEMBER CORN/DECEMBER WHEAT (CZ/WZ)

This spread trade of long December Corn/short December Wheat is intended to take advantage of the seasonal weakness in wheat which tends to extend from February until harvest in July. By spreading long corn against short wheat, the long corn will generally offset any contra-seasonal up-move in the wheat. The trade has been successful 75% of the time, carries a "Trader's Advantage" value for A of 0.94, and a rank order among the 18 trades of 13.

HISTORICAL RECORD:
1. Total Years Observed: 12
      Profit Years: 9
      Loss Years: 3
      No Trade Years: 0
2. % Profitable Years: 75%
3. % Loss Years: 25%
4. Average Profit/Year: $1587
5. Average Loss/Year: $ − 157
6. **Trader's Advantage: 0.94**
7. (Average Annual Trade Profits)/Margin Required: 1.92

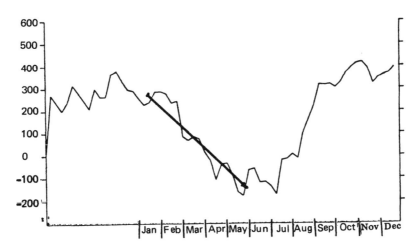

Reprinted from *"How To Profit From Seasonal Commodity Spreads"* by Jacob Bernstein
Courtesy of J. Wiley and Sons, publisher.

53

Rules For Trade #2
DECEMBER CORN/DECEMBER WHEAT (CZ/WZ)

1. Between 1/15 and 1/20, enter the spread by buying long December Corn and selling short December Wheat (equal numbers of contracts of each).

1a. Maintain a daily chart of the closing price of the spread (spread price = the difference in price between CZ and WZ).

2. After 4/10, close the spread when the price of the spread breaks (on a close basis) any 6-wk or greater trendline drawn on the daily spread chart (6TL signal). If your spread chart is a plot of CZ minus WZ, then you would watch for the 6TL signal to occur when the spread closed *under* the 6-wk trendline.

3. If the trade is still open on 6/30, close the trade that day.

Historical Results For Trade #2
DECEMBER CORN/DECEMBER WHEAT (CZ/WZ)

Margin: $600

CY	ENTRY DATE	RULE #	PRICE	EXIT DATE	RULE #	PRICE	P/L (points)	$ P/L
1971	1/15 - 1/20	1	− 1	6/30	2	− 1	0	− 90
1972	"	1	− 23	6/20	2	− 27	− 4	− 290
1973	"	1	− 105	4/12	2	− 58	+ 47	+ 2200
1974	"	1	− 208	5/15	2	− 140	+ 68	+ 3310
1975	"	1	− 112	6/18	2	− 80	+ 32	+ 1510
1976	"	1	− 108	5/15	2	− 101	+ 7	+ 260
1977	"	1	− 35	4/20	2	− 25	+ 10	+ 410
1978	"	1	− 76	6/16	2	− 76	0	− 90
1979	"	1	− 85	4/20	2	− 81	+ 4	+ 110
1980	"	1	− 182	5/ 5	2	− 148	+ 34	+ 1610
1981	"	1	− 165	4/15	2	− 98	+ 67	+ 3260
1982	"	1	− 141	6/25	2	− 107	+ 34	+ 1610

All P/L Results Include
Commission Costs

Trade #3
JULY SOYBEANS/NOVEMBER SOYBEANS (SN/SX)

This spread trade of long July/short November Soybeans is primarily a "long beans" trade to take advantage of the seasonal up-move in July beans from January to July. Due to the screening nature of the rules, it generally is not entered unless there is a strong bean market in the spring. Consequently, it was entered in only 6 of the 12 years since 1971, but for those years it was profitable 100% of the time. This trade carries a value for "A" of 1.0, and the value for "Avg. Profits/Margin Req'd" of 6.06.

HISTORICAL RECORD:
1. Total Years Observed: 12
      Profit Years: 6
      Loss Years: 0
      No Trade Years: 6
2. % Profitable Years: 100%
3. % Loss Years: 0
4. Average Profit/Year: $3936
5. Average Loss/Year: $0
6. **Trader's Advantage: 1.0**
7. (Average Annual Trade Profits)/Margin Required: 6.06

Reprinted from *"How To Profit From Seasonal Commodity Spreads"* by Jacob Bernstein
Courtesy of J. Wiley and Sons, publisher.

56

Rules For Trade #3
JULY SOYBEANS/NOVEMBER SOYBEANS (SN/SX)

To enter and exit this trade, you will have to keep a daily chart of the difference in closing prices of July and November Soybeans (SN/SX = closing price difference of SN minus SX).

1. Anytime after 1/31 and before 5/1, enter the spread long SN and short SX whenever the value of SN/SX exceeds its highs for the period 12/1 through 1/31.

2. Close the spread trade anytime after 3/10 when a 4-wk trendline or 4-wk-D drawn on the *SN chart* is broken on the downside. Note that you use the daily chart for July beans (SN) to close the trade, not the spread chart.

3. Close the trade on 7/1 if still open.

Historical Results For Trade #3
JULY SOYBEANS/NOVEMBER SOYBEANS (SN/SX)

Margin: $650

CY	ENTRY DATE	RULE #	PRICE	EXIT DATE	RULE #	PRICE	P/L (points)	$ P/L
1971	N.T.	—	—	—	—	—	—	No Trade
1972	Appx. 2/5	1	+ 23	4/27	2	+ 33	+ 10	+ 420
1973	Appx. 2/5	1	+ 95	7/ 2	3	+ 330	+ 235	+ 11,670
1974	Appx. 2/5	1	+ 22	3/26	2	+ 28	+ 6	+ 220
1975	N.T.	—	—	—	—	—	—	No Trade
1976	N.T.	—	—	—	—	—	—	No Trade
1977	Appx. 3/1	1	+ 85	4/28	2	+ 238	+ 153	+ 7,570
1978	Appx. 3/7	1	+ 34	3/29	2	+ 105	+ 71	+ 3,470
1979	Appx. 2/5	1	+ 50	3/13	2	+ 57	+ , 7	+ 270
1980	N.T.	—	—	—	—	—	—	No Trade
1981	N.T.	—	.—	—	—	—	—	No Trade
1982	N.T.	—	—	—	—	—	—	No Trade

All P/L Results Include Commission Costs

Trade #4
JUNE LIVE HOGS (LHM)

This trade of long June Hogs is designed to catch the seasonal up-move in hogs when it occurs around the middle of March. There have been three "no trade" years for this trade, but for the 9 years when it was entered, it was profitable 100% of the time. It occupies position #3, based on A = 1.0 and Avg. Profits/Margin Req'd. = 1.97.

HISTORICAL RECORD:

1. Total Years Observed: 12
    Profit Years: 9
    Loss Years: 0
    No Trade Years: 3
2. % Profitable Years: 100%
3. % Loss Years: 0
4. Average Profit/Year: $1577 (basis $50.00 LHM)
5. Average Loss/Year: $ 0
6. **Trader's Advantage: 1.0**
7. (Average Annual Trade Profits)/Margin Required: 1.97

JUNE HOGS

7 YEARS

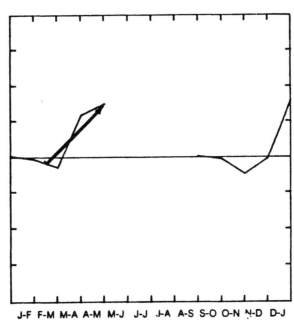

J-F F-M M-A A-M M-J J-J J-A A-S S-O O-N N-D D-J

Reprinted from *"Profits Through Seasonal Trading"* by Jack Gruschow and Courtney Smith
Courtesy of J. Wiley and Sons, publisher.

59

Rules For Trade #4
JUNE LIVE HOGS (LHM)

1. Enter this trade *only if* June Live Hogs (LHM) has traded *up* or *sideways* from early December to early February.

2. After 2/1, watch for a pull-back in prices lasting for at least two weeks; then, buy long LHM whenever a close is made which is a new season high (S.H. signal) or which breaks a 3-wk trendline (3TL signal).

3. Watch for prices for LHM to increase by 10% following entry (e.g.—if entry was made at $40.00, watch for prices to reach $44.00). This is what I call "reaching 10% profits." After 10% profits have been achieved, close the trade on a 4-wk trendline signal. Also, if still in the trade, close the trade immediately when prices reach a value 20% above the entry price.

4. Place a "double reverse stop" on a close lower than the low range in LHM for the 4-8 week period prior to entry. If activated, go short two contracts for each initial long contract, and hold for a total profit on these short contracts equal to 2-times the loss on the initial long position. Close out the short position when this condition is achieved.

5. If still long or short on 6/1, close the trade on 6/1.

Historical Results For Trade #4
JUNE LIVE HOGS (LHM)

Margin: $800

CY	ENTRY DATE	RULE #	L/S	PRICE	EXIT DATE	RULE #	PRICE	P/L (points)	P/L (%)	$ P/L (basis $50.00 LHM)
1971	3/ 3/71	2	L	19.65	6/ 1	5	20.90	+ 125	+ 6.4	+ 885
1972	3/ 6/72	2	L	26.60	6/ 1	5	28.20	+ 180	+ 6.8	+ 945
1973	2/12/73	2	L	32.60	3/15	3	37.60	+ 500	+ 15.3	+ 2225
1974	3/31/74	2	L	36.80	4/29	4	32.80	− 400 } + 400	+ 10.9	+ 1420
	4/29/74	4	S(2)	32.80	5/21	4	28.80	+ 800 }		
1975	N.T.	–	–	⋅	–	–	–	–	–	No Trade
1976	3/10/76	2	L	45.10	5/ 5	3	50.50	+ 540	+ 12.0	+ 1725
1977	3/15/77	2	L	39.10	5/16	3	46.90	+ 780	+ 20.0	+ 2920
1978	N.T.	–	–	–	–	–	–	–	–	No Trade
1979	3/21/79	2	L	52.70	3/26	4	49.10	− 360 } + 360	+ 6.8	+ 815
	3/26/79	4	S(2)	49.10	5/ 9	4	45.50	+ 720 }		
1980	2/27/80	2	L	41.25	3/20	4	39.65	− 160 } + 330	+ 8.0	+ 990
	3/20/80	4	S(2)	39.65	3/24	4	37.20	+ 490 }		
1981	N.T.	–	–	–	–	–	–	–	–	No Trade
1982	3/ 9/82	2	L	53.70	6/ 1	5	62.10	+ 840	+ 15.6	+ 2275

All P/L Results Include Commission Costs

Trade #5
JUNE GOLD (GOM)

This trade to sell short June Gold in the February-March time period does not have as much historical basis as most of the other trades. However, since gold first started trading in 1975, it has been 100% successful, without a single reversal. Its one weakness is that it does not make particularly large profits, averaging slightly over $2000 per contract per year (based on $400.00 gold). It is rank ordered 9th out of our 18 trades in the portfolio.

HISTORICAL RECORD:

1. Total Years Observed: 8
   - Profit Years: 8
   - Loss Years: 0
   - No Trade Years: 0
2. % Profitable Years: 100%
3. % Loss Years: 0
4. Average Profit/Year: $2013 (basis $400.00 GOM)
5. Average Loss/Year: $ 0
6. **Trader's Advantage: 1.0**
7. (Average Annual Trade Profits)/Margin Required: 0.58

NO SEASONAL CHARTS AVAILABLE

Rules For Trade #5
JUNE GOLD (GOM)

1. After 1/31, sell June Comex Gold on any new season low close (S. L. signal) or on a 4-wk trendline signal, whichever signal comes first. In either case, entry is made only on a "close only" basis.

2. Close the short position on the first 5-wk trendline signal (close only) which occurs following entry.

3. Place a protective stop, and close the trade if signaled, using a S.H. stop (close only), or close using 12 wk-D signal.

4. Close the trade on 6/1 if still open.

Historical Results For Trade #5
JUNE GOLD (GOM)

Margin: $3500

CY	ENTRY DATE	RULE #	L/S	PRICE	EXIT DATE	RULE #	PRICE	P/L (points)	P/L (%)	$ P/L (basis $400.00 GOM)
1975	3/ 4/75	1	S	179.30	5/13	2	167.00	+ 1230	+ 6.9	+ 2665
1976	3/ 2/76	1	S	131.75	6/ 1	2, 4	128.25	+ 350	+ 2.7	+ 980
1977	3/29/77	1	S	150.50	6/ 1	4	144.50	+ 600	+ 4.0	+ 1520
1978	3/15/78	1	S	186.50	5/10	2	174.75	+ 1175	+ 6.3	+ 2440
1979	3/ 2/79	1	S	247.50	4/23	2	244.00	+ 350	+ 1.4	+ 485
1980	2/19/80	1	S	678.00	3/ 4	2	674.00	+ 400	+ 0.6	+ 155
1981	4/ 7/81	1	S	522.00	6/ 1	4	475.00	+ 4700	+ 9.0	+ 3520
1982	2/18/82	1	S	383.00	4/ 2	2	336.50	+ 4650	+ 12.1	+ 4775

All P/L Results Include Commission Costs

64

Trade #6
JULY PLYWOOD (PWN)

This trade to sell short July Plywood in the February-March period is both reliable and profitable. It has been profitable 100% of the time since 1971, without a single reversal trade (although in one year the trade was not entered). It averages just over $1000 per contract per year (basis $200 PWN) and is ranked #6 in our portfolio of 18 seasonal trades.

HISTORICAL RECORD:
1. Total Years Observed: 12
    Profit Years: 11
    Loss Years: 0
    No Trade Years: 1
2. % Profitable Years: 100%
3. % Loss Years: 0
4. Average Profit/Year: $1015 (basis $200.00 PWN)
5. Average Loss/Year: $ 0
6. **Trader's Advantage: 1.0**
7. (Average Annual Trade Profits)/Margin Required: 1.35

JULY PLYWOOD

7 YEARS

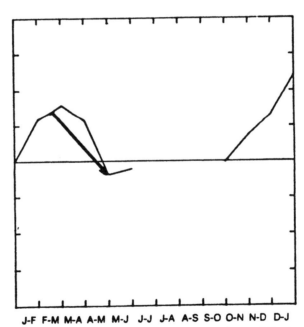

J-F F-M M-A A-M M-J J-J J-A A-S S-O O-N N-D D-J

Reprinted from *"Profits Through Seasonal Trading"* by Jack Gruschow and Courtney Smith
Courtesy of J. Wiley and Sons, publisher.   65

Rules For Trade #6
JULY PLYWOOD (PWN)

Enter this trade between 2/7 and 4/7. If you are unable to enter this trade using Rule #1, do not take the trade this year.

1. Sell short July Plywood on a close below a 6-wk trendline or below the season low for the contract (S.L. signal), whichever occurs first.

2. Protect the position with a season high (S.H.) or 12 wk-D stop. (See Chapter V for definition of 12 wk-D signal).

3. Take profits when PWN reaches a price equal to 7.5% lower than the entry price.

4. After PWN reaches a price equal to 5% lower than the entry price, close the trade on any close above a 6-wk TL (6-week trendline signal). Obviously, you would follow this signal only if it occurred before rule (3) could be used to close the trade.

5. If the trade is still open on 7/1, close on 7/1

Historical Results For Trade #6
JULY PLYWOOD (PWN)

Margin: $750

CY	ENTRY DATE	RULE #	L/S	PRICE	EXIT DATE	RULE #	PRICE	P/L (points)	P/L (%)	$ P/L (basis $200.00 PWN)
1971	3/24/71	1	S	102.00	4/26	3	94.35	+ 765	+ 7.5	+ 1075
1972	2/ 8/72	1	S	104.00	4/ 3	3	96.20	+ 780	+ 7.5	+ 1075
1973	3/26/73	1	S	158.00	4/ 7	3	146.15	+1185	+ 7.5	+ 1075
1974	4/ 3/74	1	S	132.00	4/23	3	122.10	+ 990	+ 7.5	+ 1075
1975	N.T.	–	–	–	–	–	–	–	–	No Trade
1976	3/ 4/76	1	S	158.00	5/19	3	146.15	+1185	+ 7.5	+ 1075
1977	3/29/77	1	S	205.20	5/23	3	189.80	+1540	+ 7.5	+ 1075
1978	2/23/78	1	S	209.00	4/24	4	203.25	+ 575	+ 2.8	+ 355
1979	3/12/79	1	S	206.75	6/ 7	3	191.25	+1550	+ 7.5	+ 1075
1980	2/19/80	1	S	195.00	3/24	3	180.00	+1500	+ 7.7	+ 1105
1981	2/10/81	1	S	214.50	5/14	3	197.50	+1700	+ 7.9	+ 1135
1982	2/ 8/82	1	S	191.50	3/ 8	3	177.00	+1450	+ 7.5	+ 1075

All P/L Results Include
Commission Costs

Trade #7
DECEMBER CORN (CZ)

This trade in December Corn is designed to catch and follow the seasonal Spring move in CZ, whether it be up or down. It is an unusual seasonal trade in that there are 6 years when the initial entry was a short sale and 6 years when it was entered as a long trade. Furthermore, 4 of the years had at least one reversal trade, and one year was a net loss. However, on average it is a good trade because it yields large profits, and has been profitable in 9 out of the 12 years. This is the #17 trade in the portfolio, based on a relatively low value for "A" of 0.85, but a very high value for "Average Profits/Margin Req'd." of 3.11.

HISTORICAL RECORD:

1. Total Years Observed: 12
    Profit Years: 9
    Loss Years: 3
    No Trade Years: 0
2. % Profitable Years: 75%
3. % Loss Years: 25%
4. Average Profit/Year: $2265 (basis $3.00 CZ)
5. Average Loss/Year: $ − 587
6. **Trader's Advantage: 0.85**
7. (Average Annual Trade Profits)/Margin Required: 3.11

DECEMBER CORN

11 YEARS

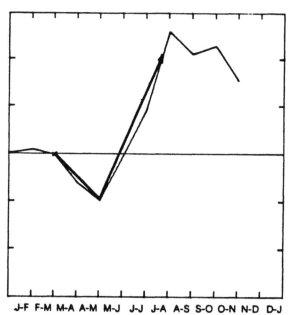

J-F F-M M-A A-M M-J J-J J-A A-S S-O O-N N-D D-J

Reprinted from *"Profits Through Seasonal Trading"* by Jack Gruschow and Courtney Smith
Courtesy of J. Wiley and Sons, publisher.

Rules For Trade #7
DECEMBER CORN (CZ)

Enter the trade using whichever of Rules (1-3) occurs first.

1. After 3/1, buy long December Corn on a season high close.

2. After 3/1, sell short December Corn on a season low close or on a close lower than the lows in CZ for the period 1/1 - 3/1.

3. After 3/1, buy long CZ on a close over an 8-wk trendline.

Close or Reverse the above positions via Rules (4-6).

4. Use any of rules (1-3) to reverse the position if the earlier trade showed a loss when a signal is given.

5. After 3/1: Sell the long CZ position, or reverse to short CZ if a loss, on an 8-wk TL signal; if short, close the position on an 8-wk TL signal, or reverse to long if the earlier trade was a loss.

6. After 5/20: Trade as in rule (5), but use a 4-wk TL to provide the signals rather than the 8-wk TL.

Keep trading using the above rules until a trade is closed yielding a profit on that trade of at least 2¢ in CZ.

69

Historical Results For Trade #7
DECEMBER CORN (CZ)

Margin: $500

CY	ENTRY DATE	RULE #	L/S	PRICE	EXIT DATE	RULE #	PRICE	P/L (points)		P/L (%)	$ P/L (basis $3.00 CZ)
1971	3/17/71	2	S	1.49¼	5/26	6	1.41¼	+ 8		+ 5.4	+ 740
1972	6/ 4/72	2	S	1.22¼	6/30	6	1.24¼	− 2 ⎫	+ 13½	+ 11.0	+ 1590
	6/30/72	6	L	1.24¼	9/27	6	1.39¾	+ 15½ ⎭			
1973	4/ 9/73	1	L	1.55	6/15	6	1.90	+ 35		+ 22.5	+ 3320
1974	4/ 2/74	2	S	2.39	5/29	3	2.48	− 9 ⎫	+ 87	+ 36.4	+ 5330
	5/29/74	3	L	2.48	8/27	6	3.44	+ 96 ⎭			
1975	3/21/75	3	L	2.65	8/26	6	3.10	+ 45		+ 17.0	+ 2480
1976	6/ 7/76	1	L	2.84	6/29	6	2.79	− 5 ⎫	− 2½	− 0.9	− 260
	6/29/76	6	S	2.79	8/13	6	2.76½	+ 2½ ⎭			
1977	4/25/77	2	S	2.56	7/ 5	6	2.36	+ 20		+ 7.8	+ 1110
1978	3/ 3/78	1	L	2.33	6/ 7	6	2.63	+ 30		+ 12.9	+ 1865
1979	4/24/79	1	L	2.68	7/23	6	3.10½	+ 42½		+ 15.9	+ 2310
1980	3/27/80	2	S	2.92	6/23	6	2.96	− 4 ⎫	+ 35	+ 12.0	+ 1670
	6/23/80	6	L	2.96	8/11	6	3.35	+ 39 ⎭			
1981	4/ 7/81	1	L	3.94	5/12	6	3.65	− 29 ⎫	− 24	− 6.1	− 1045
	5/12/81	6	S	3.65	6/12	6	3.60	+ 5 ⎭			
1982	3/ 5/82	2	S	2.87½	3/22	4	2.93½	− 6 ⎫	− 5	− 1.7	− 455
	3/22/82	4	L	2.93½	5/ 4	4	2.87	− 6½ ⎬			
	5/ 4/82	4	S	2.87	6/10	6	2.79½	+ 7½ ⎭			

All P/L Results Include
Commission Costs

Trade #8
DECEMBER COPPER (CPZ)

This trade to sell short December Copper directly follows the seasonal up-move in Copper (Trade #18 in CPN is designed to profit from the seasonal copper up-move). This trade to sell copper is generally entered in March or April. It has been profitable in 8 out of the 9 years when entered, with 3 years showing no entry. It is ranked #12 out of the 18 trades, based on a value for "A" of 0.95 and relatively modest profits of approximately $1500 per year.

HISTORICAL RECORD:

1. Total Years Observed: 12
        Profit Years: 8
        Loss Years: 1
        No Trade Years: 3
2. % Profitable Years: 89%
3. % Loss Years: 11%
4. Average Profit/Year: $1570 (basis 80¢ CPZ)
5. Average Loss/Year: $ – 80
6. **Trader's Advantage: 0.95**
7. (Average Annual Trade Profits)/Margin Required: 0.93

DECEMBER COPPER

12 YEARS

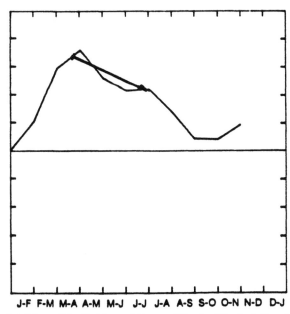

J-F F-M M-A A-M M-J J-J J-A A-S S-O O-N N-D D-J

Reprinted from *"Profits Through Seasonal Trading"* by Jack Gruschow and Courtney Smith
Courtesy of J. Wiley and Sons, publisher.

71

Rules For Trade #8
DECEMBER COPPER (CPZ)

1. To enter this trade, a run-up in December Copper prices from 1/1 to 3/15 is required such that the price on 3/15 is higher than on 2/1.

2. After 3/15, sell short CPZ on any close below a 4$^+$-TL. (4$^+$-TL means a trendline extending over at least 4-weeks plus 2 days of trading).

3. Place a protective stop at a price 2% above the high range of trading for 4 weeks prior to entry.

4. If stopped out via (3), reenter via (2) if possible, and trade via rules (3-8).

5. After a profit of 3% is achieved (price of CPZ declines 3% from the entry price), move the protective stop (intraday) in rule (3) to assure a 1% profit, or to 4-wk-D to close out the position.

6. After a profit of 10% is reached (prices decline by 10% from entry), move the stop to assure a 4% profit (place the stop 4% below entry price), or close the position on any 4-wk-D signal.

7. If 15% profits are reached (prices decline by 15% from entry), close the position immediately.

8. After being in the trade for 6 weeks, move the stop for rule (3) to the original entry price.

9. Do not enter any new short positions after 6/1.

Historical Results For Trade #8
DECEMBER COPPER (CPZ)

Margin: $1500

CY	ENTRY DATE	RULE #	L/S	PRICE	EXIT DATE	RULE #	PRICE	P/L (points)	P/L (%)	$ P/L (basis 80¢ CPZ)
1971	4/26/71	2	S	56.50	6/ 1	7	48.05	+ 845	+ 15.0	+ 2920
1972	3/22/72	2	S	54.00	8/21	6	50.50	+ 350	+ 6.5	+ 1215
1973	4/30/73	2	S	65.00	5/ 9	5	65.00	0	0	– 80
1974	4/ 8/74	2	S	106.50	4/19	3	119.50	– 1300 } + 500	+ 4.7	+ 780
	5/13/74	4	S	119.00	5/23	7	101.15	+1800 }		
1975	4/ 4/75	2	S	63.10	6/30	6	58.00	+ 510	+ 8.1	+ 1535
1976	4/29/76	2	S	73.20	5/ 6	5	72.50	+ 70	+ 1.0	+ 120
1977	3/25/77	2	S	73.80	5/23	7	62.75	+1105	+ 15.0	+ 2920
1978	4/13/78	2	S	63.50	5/ 2	5	62.85	+ 65	+ 1.0	+ 120
1979	4/18/79	2	S	93.25	7/ 2	7	79.25	+1400	+ 15.0	+ 2920
1980	N.T.	–	–	–	–	–	–	–	–	No Trade
1981	N.T.	–	–	–	–	–	–	–	–	No Trade
1982	N.T.	–	–	–	–	–	–	–	–	No Trade

All P/L Results Include
Commission Costs

73

Trade #9
JULY LIVE HOGS/JULY PORK BELLIES (LHN/PBN)

This is a seasonal spread trade which seeks to take advantage of the tendency for July Bellies to go down from April into July, while July Hogs generally continue to go up. To even out the contract sizes, the trade uses 1½ contracts long for the hogs, spread against a single contract of bellies sold short. The trade has been profitable 9 out of the 10 years it was entered, with two years showing no entry. It ranks #18 out of the 18 trades in the portfolio.

HISTORICAL RECORD:

1. Total Years Observed: 12
    Profit Years: 9
    Loss Years: 1
    No Trade Years: 2
2. % Profitable Years: 90%
3. % Loss Years: 10%
4. Average Profit/Year: $2590
5. Average Loss/Year: $ −1620
6. **Trader's Advantage: 0.85**
7. (Average Annual Trade Profits)/Margin Required: 1.08

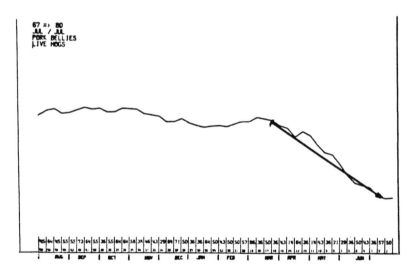

Reprinted from *"How to Profit From Seasonal Commodity Spreads"* by Jacob Bernstein
Courtesy of J. Wiley and Sons, publisher.

Rules For Trade #9
JULY LIVE HOGS/JULY PORK BELLIES (LHN/PBN)

Maintain a daily chart of the price difference of July Live Hogs (LHN) minus July Pork Bellies (PBN). Trade signals #1 and #2 are made from this chart. Also, maintain a daily bar chart for PBN since trade rule #3 uses this chart.

1. After 2/26, when the spread price breaks the highs recorded on the spread chart during February, initiate the spread trade long 1½ contracts LHN and short 1 contract PBN. After 3/31, enter the trade when the spread price exceeds the highs recorded in March. Require the spread to close above the target price by 30-50 points for entry.

This trade uses 1½ contracts of LHN spread against 1 contract of PBN in order to even the two sides of the spread (the live hog contract contains 300,000 lbs. per contract, whereas the pork belly contract contains 380,000 lbs. per contract). In fact, the trade works almost as well if you spread equal numbers of contracts of LHN and PBN, but it works better the way I have detailed it.

2. Protect the trade with a stop at the lows for the spread recorded during the period February-March.

3. Close the trade in June whenever PBN closes above a 4-wk trendline or above the season high on the PBN daily bar chart. If the trade is still open on 7/1, close the trade on 7/1.

Historical Results For Trade #9
JULY LIVE HOGS/JULY PORK BELLIES (LHN/PBN)

Margin: $2000

CY	ENTRY DATE	PRICE	EXIT DATE	PRICE	$ P/L
1971	3/ 5/71	− 550	7/ 1	− 200	+ 1560
1972	5/16/72	− 950	6/ 8	− 550	+ 1300
1973	4/ 5/73	− 1680	6/26	− 1700	+ 380
1974	3/ 2/74	− 950	6/20	− 300	+ 850
1975	N.T.	−	−	−	No Trade
1976	N.T.	−	−	−	No Trade
1977	3/10/77	− 1380	6/27	− 1000	+ 1725
1978	4/ 7/78	− 2600	7/ 1	− 30	+ 9370
1979	3/ 8/79	− 940	6/ 8	− 140	+ 2000
1980	4/14/80	+ 100	6/11	+ 720	+ 2370
1981	3/ 2/81	− 250	7/ 1	+ 660	+ 3770
1982	3/16/82	− 1735	4/23	+ 2250	− 1620

Trade #10
DECEMBER SOYBEAN OIL (BOZ)

This trade in December Soybean Oil is both highly reliable and highly profitable. It is generally a long trade entered after May 1 to catch the strong seasonal move into Fall. If, however, new season lows are registered during this period, the trade is entered as a short sale. Historically, it has been entered long nine times out of the last twelve years, with 3 of those years requiring a trade reversal to short. It ranks as our #11 trade, based on a value for the "Trader's Advantage" of 0.95 and a ratio of profits to margin requirements of 2.16.

HISTORICAL RECORD:

1. Total Years Observed: 12
    Profit Years: 11
    Loss Years: 1
    No Trade Years 0
2. % Profitable Years: 92%
3. % Loss Years: 8%
4. Average Profit/Year: $2410 (basis 20¢ BOZ)
5. Average Loss/Year: $ – 680
6. **Trader's Advantage: 0.95**
7. (Average Annual Trade Profits)/Margin Required: 2.16

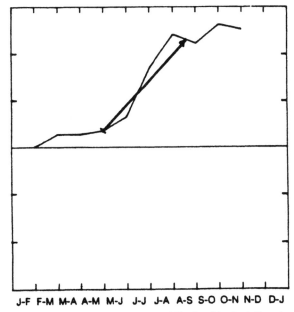

J-F F-M M-A A-M M-J J-J J-A A-S S-O O-N N-D D-J

Reprinted from *"Profits Through Seasonal Trading"* by Jack Gruschow and Courtney Smith
Courtesy of J. Wiley and Sons, publisher.

Rules For Trade #10
DECEMBER SOYBEAN OIL (BOZ)

1. After 5/1, buy a season high close of December Soybean Oil.

2. After 5/1, buy a close which breaks a 6-wk trendline.

3. After 5/1, sell a season low close.

4. Close long positions via a 5^+-wk trendline; reverse the position to short if the long trade is closed at a loss. (A 5^+-wk trendline is a trendline extending across at least 5-weeks plus 2 days of trading on the daily bar chart).

5. Close short positions via a 5^+-wk trendline signal.

6a. Do not close any *long* position within the first month after entry, except by S.L. signal or condition (b) below.

 b. If entry is via S.H. signal, put a reverse stop at a distance below the old S.H. price equal to 200% of the difference between the old S.H. price and the price of the entry for the long BOZ trade.

7. After profits of 40% are reached (on close), close the trade on a 1LC3 signal (if long), or a 1HC3 signal (if short). If profits of 60% are reached (intraday), close the trade.

8. Close any open position on 12/1.

9. Keep trading via rules (1) - (6) until the last trade is a profitable trade.

Historical Results For Trade #10
DECEMBER SOYBEAN OIL (BOZ)

Margin: $1000

CY	ENTRY DATE	RULE #	L/S	PRICE	EXIT DATE	RULE #	PRICE	P/L (points)	P/L (%)	$ P/L (basis 20¢ BOZ)
1971	5/ 5/71	2	L	10.40	7/26	4	13.10	+ 270	+ 26.0	+ 3060
1972	6/14/72	3	S	10.42	8/ 4	5	10.30	+ 12	+ 1.2	+ 80
1973	5/18/73	1	L	13.00	7/31	7	20.80	+ 780	+ 60.0	+ 7140
1974	6/17/74	1	L	25.10	7/30	7	40.16	+1506	+ 60.0	+ 7140
1975	5/ 5/75	3	S	19.80	6/18	5	18.80	+ 100	+ 5.1	+ 550
1976	5/24/76	2	L	17.00	7/19	7	22.05	+ 505	+ 29.7	+ 3505
1977	5/26/77	1	L	28.55	6/ 9	6	27.55	− 100 } + 590	+ 20.7	+ 2420
	6/ 9/77	6	S	27.55	8/ 3	5	20.65	+ 690 }		
1978	5/23/78	1	L	24.20	6/ 9	6	23.45	− 75 } + 60	+ 2.5	+ 180
	6/ 9/78	6	S	23.45	7/26	5	22.10	+ 135 }		
1979	5/21/79	1	L	26.25	7/27	4	26.40	+ 15	+ 0.6	+ 10
1980	5/ 9/80	2	L	22.40	9/25	4	26.60	+ 420	+ 18.8	+ 2190
1981	5/12/81	3	S	25.50	6/16	5	24.85	+ 65	+ 2.5	+ 240
1982	7/ 2/82	3	S	19.25	7/13	2	19.65	− 40 }	− 4.1	− 680
	7/13/82	2	L	19.65	7/30	6	18.75	− 90 } − 80		
	7/29/82	4	S	18.75	8/23	5	18.25	+ 50 }		

All P/L Results Include Commission Costs

79

Trade #11
DECEMBER COCOA (CCZ)

This seasonal trade in December Cocoa is based on the tendency of this market to advance from May until the end of the year. It is always entered as a long trade. However, in 3 out of 12 years a subsequent short position was taken. It has been profitable 11 out of the last 12 years. It is ranked #15 in our portfolio of 18 trades.

HISTORICAL RECORD:

1. Total Years Observed: 12
    Profit Years: 11
    Loss Years: 1
    No Trade Years: 0
2. % Profitable Years: 92%
3. % Loss Years: 8%
4. Average Profit/Year: $3480 (basis $2000 CCZ)
5. Average Loss/Year: $ – 1500
6. **Trader's Advantage: 0.92**
7. (Average Annual Trade Profits)/Margin Required: 1.52

DECEMBER COCOA

11 YEARS

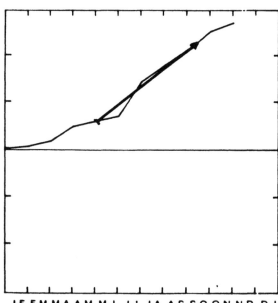

J-F F-M M-A A-M M-J J-J J-A A-S S-O O-N N-D D-J

Reprinted from *"Profits Through Seasonal Trading"* by Jack Gruschow and Courtney Smith
Courtesy of J. Wiley and Sons, publisher.

Rules For Trade #11
DECEMBER COCOA (CCZ)

1. Watch for a good downtrend from March-May in December Cocoa, and buy long on a close above a 6-wk trendline after 5/1 and before 8/1.

2. Buy long CCZ on any S.H. close after 5/15. If this signal occurs in May or June, do not take the trade unless there is a 1-week or longer consolidation in trading prior to making the season high. Do not use this rule after 8/1.

3. Protect long positions with a *reverse stop* at the trading lows for the period April 1 to entry date. If activated, hold the short position for one of the following conditions (whichever is greater): a decline in prices by 4% from the short position entry price; a 100 point decline in price; or, a drop in price of 2-times the prior loss.

   Also protect long positions via 6TL signal in rule (4).

4a. Close long positions when 30% profit is touched (i.e.—prices increase by 30% from the entry price).

   b. After prices reach the 25% profit level, close long CCZ positions on the first close lower than the trading range of the prior three days of trading. Move this "close only stop" each day based on the prior three days' trading ranges.

   c. After reaching 10% profits, but prior to reaching either 25% or 30% profits, close the trade on a 6-wk TL signal.

5. Close the CCZ trade on 12/1 if it is still open.

81

Historical Results For Trade #11
DECEMBER COCOA (CCZ)

Margin: $2000

CY	ENTRY DATE	RULE #	L/S	PRICE	EXIT DATE	RULE #	PRICE	P/L (points)	P/L (%)	$ P/L (basis $2000 CCZ)
1971	6/ 8/71	1	L	23.60	8/17	4(c)	25.70	+ 200	+ 8.5	+ 1600
1972	5/ 8/72	2	L	28.20	9/19	4(c)	31.20	+ 300	+ 10.6	+ 2035
1973	6/15/73	2	L	56.50	7/23	4(a)	73.50	+ 1700	+ 30.0	+ 5910
1974	7/12/74	1	L	68.00	9/13	4(c)	76.00	+ 800	+ 11.8	+ 2265
1975	6/30/75	1	L	43.00	7/22	4(a)	55.90	+ 1290	+ 30.0	+ 5910
1976	6/ 4/76	2	L	77.50	7/13	4(c)	85.00	+ 750	+ 9.7	+ 1845
1977	5/18/77	1	L	159.50	7/20	4(b)	197.00	+ 3750	+ 23.5	+ 4610
1978	6/19/78	1	L	132.00	9/11	4(a)	171.60	+ 3940	+ 30.0	+ 5910
1979	5/ 1/79	1	L	152.00	7/11	3	143.25	− 875 } + 875	+ 5.8	+ 970
	7/11/79	3	S	143.25	10/24	3	125.75	+ 1750 }		
1980	7/14/80	1	L	2425	7/30	3	2225	− 170 } + 170	+ 7.0	+ 1310
	7/30/80	3	S	2225	12/ 1	3	1915	+ 340 }		
1981	6/26/81	1	L	1690	7/29	4(a)	2197	+ 57	+ 30.0	+ 5910
1982	6/23/82	1	L	1510	7/19	3	1410	− 100 } − 100	− 6.6	− 1500
	7/19/82	3	S	1410	12/ 1	5	1410	0 }		

All P/L Results Include Commission Costs

Trade #12
DECEMBER OATS (OZ)

This trade to sell short December Oats in June-July shows profits in 10 out of the last 12 years, in spite of the fact that the seasonal data for "nearest futures" provided by Gruschow and Smith (see bibliography) does not indicate a strong seasonal tendency for the trade. This non-seasonal characteristic is at least partially reflected in the fact that the trade has been reversed to long in 4 out of the 12 years studied. Even so, it scores adequately in our rank order. Based on a value for "A" of 0.93 it is ranked 14 out of 18, due to the relatively large profits which it often achieves.

HISTORICAL RECORD:

1. Total Years Observed: 12
    Profit Years: 10
    Loss Years: 2
    No Trade Years: 0
2. % Profitable Years: 83%
3. % Loss Years: 17%
4. Average Profit/Year: $1138 (basis $1.80 OZ)
5. Average Loss/Year: $−217
6. **Trader's Advantage: 0.93**
7. (Average Annual Trade Profits)/Margin Required: 1.82

OATS NEAREST FUTURES
4 YEARS

J-F F-M M-A A-M M-J J-J J-A A-S S-O O-N N-D D-J

Reprinted from *"Profits Through Seasonal Trading"* by Jack Gruschow and Courtney Smith
Courtesy of J. Wiley and Sons, publisher.

83

Rules For Trade #12
DECEMBER OATS (OZ)

1. After 5/30, sell short December Oats on any close that breaks a 4-wk trendline.

2. After 5/30, sell short OZ on any new season low close.

3. If unable to enter via (1) or (2) prior to 7/1, sell short OZ on the first close on or after 7/1 which is lower than the close on the prior 3 trading days.

4. Protect the short OZ position with a *reverse stop* (close only) placed 5% above the entry price for the short OZ position.

5. After 8/1, close any short OZ position on the first close higher than the close of the prior day. Update this stop daily.

6. After 8/1, close any long OZ position on a close that breaks a 5-wk trendline.

Historical Results For Trade #12
DECEMBER OATS (OZ)

Margin: $500

CY	ENTRY DATE	RULE #	L/S	PRICE	EXIT DATE	RULE #	PRICE	P/L (points)	P/L (%)	$ P/L (basis $1.80 OZ)
1971	6/21/71	1	S	.74	8/ 3	5	65½	+ 8½	+ 11.4	+ 985
1972	7/12/72	3	S	.74½	8/ 7	4	79	− 4½ }	− 1.3	− 220
	8/ 7/72	4	L	.79	9/ 7	6	82½	+ 3½ } − 1		
1973	6/28/73	2	S	1.00	7/11	4	1.05	− 5 }	+ 32.0	+ 2780
	7/11/73	4	L	1.05	8/20	6	1.42	+ 37 } + 32		
1974	7/10/74	1	S	1.55	7/15	4	1.64	− 9 }	− 1.3	− 215
	7/15/74	4	L	1.64	8/12	6	1.71	+ 7 } − 2		
1975*	7/18/75	1	S	1.44½	7/75	4	1.52	− 7½ }	+ 4.8	+ 335
	7/25/75	4	L	1.52	8/27	6	1.66½	+ 14½ } + 7		
1976*	7/ 8/76	3	S	1.88	8/ 4	5	1.64	+ 24	+ 12.8	+ 1100
1977	6/ 7/77	2	S	1.52	8/ 3	5	1.12½	+ 39½	+ 26.0	+ 2290
1978	6/ 1/78	1	S	1.58	8/ 3	5	1.34	+ 24	+ 15.8	+ 1315
1979	7/ 5/79	1	S	1.82¼	8/ 3	5	1.52	+ 30¼	+ 16.6	+ 1440
1980	7/17/80	1	S	1.99½	8/ 5	5	1.94	+ 5½	+ 2.8	+ 200
1981	6/29/81	1	S	2.01	8/ 6	5	1.99½	+ 1½	+ 0.7	+ 15
1982	7/14/82	1	S	1.76	8/10	5	1.57	+ 19	+ 10.8	+ 920

All P/L Results Include Commission Costs

*Data From OU Rather Than OZ

85

Trade #13
DECEMBER WHEAT (WZ)

This trade to buy December Wheat in late summer is clearly one of the most reliable in the portfolio. It is based on extremely strong historical trade tendencies. Every time the trade has been entered since 1971 it has been correct (there were five years when the trade was not entered). For the 7 years it was entered, it was never reversed and profits averaged over $3500 per contract per year. It carries the rank order of #2 out of the 18 trades in the portfolio.

HISTORICAL RECORD:

1. Total Years Observed: 12
   Profit Years: 7
   Loss Years: 0
   No Trade Years: 5
2. % Profitable Years: 100%
3. % Loss Years: 0%
4. Average Profit/Year: $3660 (basis $3.80 WZ)
5. Average Loss/Year: $0
6. **Trader's Advantage: 1.0**
7. (Average Annual Trade Profits)/Margin Required: 3.67

DECEMBER WHEAT

11 YEARS

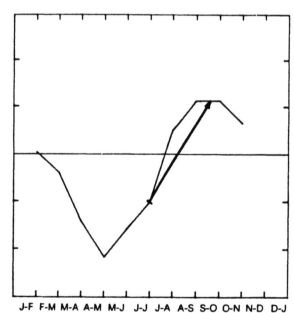

J-F F-M M-A A-M M-J J-J J-A A-S S-O O-N N-D D-J

Reprinted from *"Profits Through Seasonal Trading"* by Jack Gruschow and Courtney Smith
Courtesy of J. Wiley and Sons, publisher.

Rules For Trade #13
DECEMBER WHEAT (WZ)

1. After 6/30 and before 10/5, buy long December Wheat when the price exceeds (close only) the highs of the prior 30 days of trading.

2. Place a protective stop (close only) at the lows of the prior 30 days of trading. Move this stop on a daily basis so that you are always considering the immediately prior 30 days.

3. Close the long position when WZ closes below a 6-wk trendline; or, close on 12/1 if the trade is still open.

Historical Results For Trade #13
DECEMBER WHEAT (WZ)

Margin: $1000

CY	ENTRY DATE	RULE #	L/S	PRICE	EXIT DATE	RULE #	PRICE	P/L (points)	P/L (%)	$ P/L (basis $3.80 WZ)
1971	N.T.	–	–	–	–	–	–	–	–	No Trade
1972	7/ 7/72	1	L	1.56	10/ 4	3	2.08	+ 52	+ 33.3	+ 6,270
1973	7/20/73	1	L	3.08	9/ 3	3	4.80	+ 172	+ 55.8	+ 10,545
1974	9/30/74	1	L	4.90	10/28	3	5.13	+ 23	+ 4.7	+ 830
1975	7/ 9/75	1	L	3.47	9/ 2	3	4.15	+ 68	+ 19.6	+ 3,660
1976	N.T.	–	–	–	–	–	–	–	–	No Trade
1977	9/ 9/77	1	L	2.38½	12/ 1	3	2.67	+ 28½	+ 11.9	+ 2,205
1978	8/24/78	1	L	3.31	10/20	3	3.38	+ 7	+ 2.1	+ 335
1979	N.T.	–	–	–	–	–	–	–	–	No Trade
1980	7/ 2/80	1	L	4.67	11/11	3	5.12	+ 45	+ 9.7	+ 1,765
1981	N.T.	–	–	–	–	–	–	–	–	No Trade
1982	N.T.	–	–	–	–	–	–	–	–	No Trade

All P/L Results Include
Commission Costs

88

Trade #14
NOVEMBER SOYBEANS (SX)

This trade to buy November Soybeans in August does not appear obvious on most seasonal trading charts. However, it was entered in 10 of the last 12 years, and was profitable every year that it was entered. It ranks 4th in our portfolio, based on a value for "A" of 1.0 and an average annual profit equal to 150% of the margin required for the trade.

HISTORICAL RECORD:

1. Total Years Observed: 12
    Profit Years: 10
    Loss Years: 0
    No Trade Years: 2
2. % Profitable Years: 100%
3. % Loss Years: 0
4. Average Profit/Year: $2622 (basis $7.00 SX)
5. Average Loss/Year: $0
6. **Trader's Advantage: 1.0**
7. (Average Annual Trade Profits)/Margin Required: 1.50

NOVEMBER SOYBEANS

11 YEARS

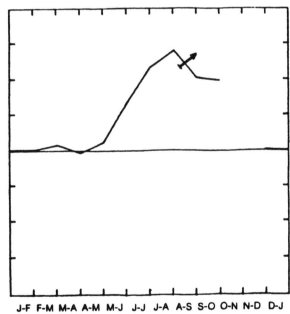

J-F F-M M-A A-M M-J J-J J-A A-S S-O O-N N-D D-J

Reprinted from *"Profits Through Seasonal Trading"* by Jack Gruschow and Courtney Smith
Courtesy of J. Wiley and Sons, publisher.

Rules For Trade #14
NOVEMBER SOYBEANS (SX)

Do not enter this trade if the trend in November Soybeans has been steadily down from January through August (as in 1981 and 1982).

1. After 8/3, buy long November Soybeans on a close above any of the following: a) 2.5 week trendline
    b) season high
    c) 4-week Donchian signal

2. Close the long SX position on any of the following:
    a) If entry was via rule 1(a)—close the long on a 60% retracement of the down-move upon which the 2.5-wk TL was based.
    b) If entry was via rule 1(b) or 1(c)—close the long when prices reach 108% of the entry price.
    c) Close on 10/31, if still open.

3. Place a protective stop (close only) on the long SX position at 2¢ below the lows registered for 4-weeks prior to entry.

Historical Results For Trade #14
NOVEMBER SOYBEANS (SX)

Margin $1750

CY	ENTRY DATE	RULE #	L/S	PRICE	EXIT DATE	RULE #	PRICE	P/L (points)	P/L (%)	$ P/L (basis $7.00 SX)
1971	8/17/71	1	L	3.20	8/19	2a	3.32	+ 12	+ 3.8	+ 1265
1972	8/ 4/72	1	L	3.33	10/30	2b	3.59	+ 46	+ 13.8	+ 4765
1973	8/10/73	1	L	8.49	8/14	2b	9.17	+ 68	+ 8.0	+ 2735
1974	9/ 9/74	1	L	7.35	9/26	2a	8.21	+ 86	+ 11.7	+ 4030
1975	9/10/75	1	L	5.65	9/17	2a	6.05	+ 40	+ 7.1	+ 2420
1976	8/ 4/76	1	L	6.30	9/ 2	2a	7.08	+ 78	+ 12.4	+ 4270
1977	8/24/77	1	L	5.20	10/31	2c	5.51	+ 31	+ 6.0	+ 2020
1978	8/11/78	1	L	6.08	8/24	2a	6.51	+ 43	+ 7.1	+ 2410
1979	8/14/79	1	L	7.14	9/18	2a	7.45	+ 31	+ 4.3	+ 1455
1980	8/25/80	1	L	7.85	8/29	2a	8.05	+ 20	+ 2.6	+ 850
1981	N.T.	–	–	–	–	–	–	–	–	No Trade
1982	N.T.	–	–	–	–	–	–	–	–	No Trade

All P/L Results Include
Commission Costs

91

Trade #15
DECEMBER GOLD (GOZ)

This trade is like #5 in GOM in that we do not have very much historical data. However, for the eight years since 1975 when trading first started in this contract, this trade has returned a profit 100% of the time. It calls for the purchase of a long position in December Gold during the August-September period. Its profits are quite good (over $4500 per contract per year, based on $400 gold) resulting in a rank order in our portfolio of #6 out of 18.

HISTORICAL RECORD:

1. Total Years Observed: 8
   Profit Years: 8
   Loss Years: 0
   No Trade Years: 0
2. % Profitable Years: 100%
3. % Loss Years: 0
4. Average Profit/Year: $4650 (basis $400.00 GOZ)
5. Average Loss/Year: $0
6. **Trader's Advantage: 1.0**
7. (Average Annual Trade Profits)/Margin Required: 1.33

NO SEASONAL CHARTS AVAILABLE

Rules For Trade #15
DECEMBER GOLD (GOZ)

Watch for "bottoming action" in December Comex Gold in the August-September period. Then, buy long GOZ after 8/1 on one of the following signals:

B1. "Significant bottoming" reversal action (e.g.—the island reversal on 9/24/75 and the big daily reversals on 8/25/76 and 8/29/78).
B2. Prices close above a 5-wk trendline.
B3. Prices close above the season high, or close above the high range for the prior 4-weeks of trading.

Protect the long position via:

P1. Place a protective sell stop (close only) at the lows of the 4-weeks of trading prior to entry.

Take profits via the following signals:

S1. Sell the long GOZ position on a close that closes below a 5-week trendline.
S2. After the price of GOZ closes above the entry price by 20%, close the long position on the first close lower than the lowest close for the prior 3-days of trading. Move this stop daily until the position is closed.

Historical Results For Trade #15
DECEMBER GOLD (GOZ)

Margin $3500

CY	ENTRY DATE	RULE #	L/S	PRICE	EXIT DATE	RULE #	PRICE	P/L (points)	P/L (%)	$ P/L (basis $400.00 GOZ)
1975	9/24/75	B1	L	137.00	11/11	S1	144.00	+ 700	+ 5.1	+ 1,960
1976	8/25/76	B1	L	106.00	11/15	S2	136.50	+ 3050	+ 28.8	+ 11,430
1977	9/ 2/77	B3	L	150.50	11/10	S1	163.50	+ 1300	+ 8.6	+ 3,375
1978	8/29/78	B1	L	211.50	11/ 2	S1	223.00	+ 1150	+ 5.4	+ 2,080
1979	8/23/79	B3	L	324.00	11/ 3	S2	403.00	+ 7900	+ 24.4	+ 9,670
1980	8/20/80	B2	L	647.00	9/29	S1	680.00	+ 3300	+ 5.1	+ 1,960
1981	8/11/81	B2	L	430.00	9/25	S1	442.00	+ 1200	+ 2.8	+ 1,035
1982	8/20/82	B3	L	395.00	9/10	S2	452.00	+ 5700	+ 14.4	+ 5,680

All P/L Results Include
Commission Costs

Trade #16
JULY COTTON (CTN)

This trade is designed to generally take a long position in July Cotton sometime during the months from October to March. It has profited 100% of the time since 1971, with the profits being made on long positions in 7 of the 12 years, and on short positions in the other 5 years. It ranks #7 in our portfolio of 18 trades, based on a value for "A" of 1.0 and annual profits equal to 129% of the margin required.

HISTORICAL RECORD:

1. Total Years Observed: 12
   Profit Years: 12
   Loss Years: 0
   No Trade Years: 0
2. % Profitable Years: 100%
3. % Loss Years: 0
4. Average Profit/Year: $2570 (basis 70¢ CTN)
5. Average Loss/Year: $0
6. **Trader's Advantage: 1.0**
7. (Average Annual Trade Profits)/Margin Required: 1.29

JULY COTTON

10 YEARS

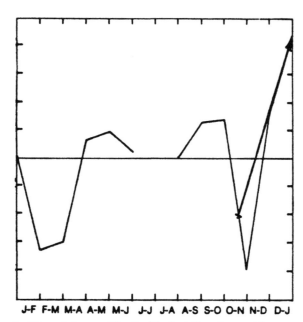

J-F F-M M-A A-M M-J J-J J-A A-S S-O O-N N-D D-J

Reprinted from *"Profits Through Seasonal Trading"* by Jack Gruschow and Courtney Smith
Courtesy of J. Wiley and Sons, publisher.

Rules For Trade #16
JULY COTTON (CTN)

1. After 10/1, buy long July Cotton on any close higher than the season high for CTN, or on any close that breaks a 10-week trendline.

2. After 10/1, sell short CTN on any close under the season lows for the contract, or on any close that breaks a 10-week trendline.

3. Protect these positions as follows:

   a) If the trade is about to close at prices at least 2% above the entry price, use a 7-wk TL signal to close.
   b) If the trade is about to close at prices which are not at least 2% above entry price, use an 8-wk TL signal to *reverse* the trade.

4. If possible, hold the long or short position entered via (1), (2) or (3b) until prices increase by 10% (if long), or decrease by 10% (if short). When this occurs, close the position.

5. If the trade is open on 7/1, close on that day.

Historical Results For Trade #16
JULY COTTON (CTN)

Margin: $2000

CY	ENTRY DATE	RULE #	L/S	PRICE	EXIT DATE	RULE #	PRICE	P/L (points)	P/L (%)	$ P/L (basis 70¢ CTN)
1971	1/18/71	1	L	27.35	3/15/71	3	27.30	− 5 }		
	3/15/71	3	S	27.30	4/12/71	3	28.60	− 130 } + 170	+ 6.2	+ 1875
	4/12/71	3	L	28.60	5/18/71	4	31.45	+ 305 }		
1972	11/23/71	1	L	33.50	1/ 3/72	4	36.85	+ 335	+ 10.0	+ 3400
1973	10/30/72	1	L	29.50	11/15/72	4	32.45	+ 295	+ 10.0	+ 3400
1974	12/10/73	1	L	77.00	12/28/73	4	84.70	+ 770	+ 10.0	+ 3400
1975	10/11/74	2	S	50.80	11/12/74	4	45.50	+ 530	+ 10.4	+ 3540
1976	12/11/75	1	L	61.00	1/15/76	3	61.50	+ 50 }		
	1/15/76	3	S	61.50	5/ 3/76	1	64.50	− 300 } + 395	+ 6.5	+ 2075
	5/ 3/76	1	L	64.50	6/ 4/76	4	70.95	+ 645 }		
1977	10/ 4/76	1	L	80.70	12/13/76	3	77.50	− 320 }		
	12/13/76	3	S	77.60	1/12/77	4	69.40	+ 840 } + 520	+ 6.4	+ 2055
1978	10/25/77	2	S	53.90	12/15/77	3	53.40	+ 50 }		
	12/15/77	3	L	53.40	2/ 6/78	4	58.75	+ 535 } + 585	+ 10.8	+ 3600
1979	10/ 2/78	1	L	70.00	11/13/78	3	72.20	+ 220	+ 3.1	+ 1000
1980	11/ 7/79	1	L	71.00	1/ 2/80	4	78.10	+ 710	+ 10.0	+ 3400
1981	1/26/81	2	S	89.70	7/ 1/81	5	84.40	+ 530	+ 5.9	+ 1970
1982	11/ 9/81	2	S	69.70	12/23/81	3	67.20	+ 250	+ 3.6	+ 1150

All P/L Results Include Commission Costs

97

Trade #17
FEBRUARY PORK BELLIES (PBG)

This trade is always entered by going long February Pork Bellies shortly after the 1st of November. It is based on the strong seasonal tendency for February bellies to bottom in November. The trading rules stipulate, however, that this trade should be reversed to short if the up-move does not materialize. Just such a reversal occurred in five of the 12 years that the trade was entered. Overall, the trade returned profits 11 out of the 12 years entered. It ranks 10th in our portfolio and it has returned profits of over $2500 per contract per year (based on 70¢ bellies).

HISTORICAL RECORD:
1. Total Years Observed: 12
        Profit Years: 11
        Loss Years: 1
        No Trade Years: 0
2. % Profitable Years: 92%
3. % Loss Years: 8%
4. Average Profit/Year: $2675 (basis 70¢ PBG)
5. Average Loss/Year: $ – 270
6. **Trader's Advantage: 0.98**
7. (Average Annual Trade Profits)/Margin Required: 1.22

FEBRUARY PORK BELLIES

10 YEARS

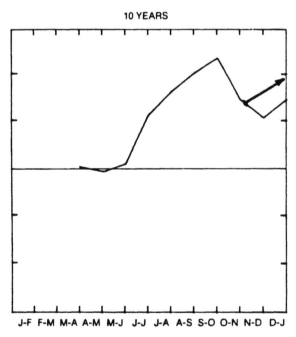

J-F F-M M-A A-M M-J J-J J-A A-S S-O O-N N-D D-J

Reprinted from *"Profits Through Seasonal Trading"* by Jack Gruschow and Courtney Smith
Courtesy of J. Wiley and Sons, publisher.

Rules For Trade #17
FEBRUARY PORK BELLIES (PBG)

Entry:

1. After 10/30, buy long February Pork Bellies on the first day when the close is higher than the closes of any of the prior three trading days. Update this entry technique on a daily basis until entry is made.

Exit:

2. Sell the long PBG position when the price reaches 110% of the entry price (except for those cases when rule (3) applies).

3. If, prior to achieving 110% of entry price, the price of PBG should close above the highs of the prior 8-weeks of trading, then hold the long PBG position until prices *exceed* 110% of the entry price. Then close the trade on a 4-wk trendline signal (close only).

4. Employ a reverse stop on any close under an 8-wk trendline or 8-wk-D signal. If reversed to short, close the short position on a 4-wk TL signal (close only).
(Note: Use this rule only if the trade will close at a loss of more than 50 points).

5. Close the trade on 2/1 if still open.

Historical Results For Trade #17
FEBRUARY PORK BELLIES (PBG)

Margin $2000

CY	ENTRY DATE	RULE #	L/S	PRICE	EXIT DATE	RULE #	PRICE	P/L (points)		P/L (%)	$ P/L (basis 70¢ PBG)
1971	11/ 2/70	1	L	30.20	11/23/70	4	29.00	− 120 }	+ 30	+ 1.0	+ 130
	11/23/70	4	S	29.00	12/16/70	4	27.50	+150 }			
1972	11/ 4/71	1	L	30.90	2/ 1/72	3	40.40	+ 950		+ 30.7	+ 8090
1973	11/ 1/72	1	L	48.00	1/24/73	3	51.30	+ 330		+ 6.9	+ 1740
1974	11/ 1/73	1	L	65.10	11/10/73	2	71.60	+ 650		+ 10.0	+ 2580
1975	11/15/74	1	L	61.00	12/20/74	3	67.10	+ 610		+ 10.0	+ 2580
1976	11/ 5/75	1	L	83.00	11/28/75	4	78.00	− 500 }	+ 100	+ 1.2	+ 160
	11/28/75	4	S	78.00	12/22/75	4	72.00	+ 600 }			
1977	11/ 4/76	1	L	47.00	1/ 7/77	3	51.70	+ 470		+ 10.0	+ 2580
1978	11/ 4/77	1	L	50.00	1/18/78	3	61.00	+1100		+ 22.0	+ 5770
1979	11/ 8/78	1	L	65.30	12/11/78	4	63.00	− 230 }	+ 320	+ 4.9	+ 1130
	12/11/78	4	S	63.00	1/ 2/79	4	57.50	+ 550 }			
1980	11/ 5/79	1	L	48.45	11/26/79	3	52.00	+ 355		+ 7.3	+ 1860
1981	11/17/80	1	L	69.20	12/ 8/80	4	65.50	− 370 }	+ 780	+ 11.3	+ 2830
	12/ 8/80	4	S	65.50	1/22/81	4	54.00	+1150 }			
1982	11/ 4/81	1	L	68.90	11/23/81	4	62.20	− 770 }	− 30	− 0.4	− 270
	11/23/81	4	S	62.20	12/17/81	4	55.80	+ 740 }			

All P/L Results Include Commission Costs

100

Trade #18
JULY COPPER (CPN)

This long trade in July Copper has a beautiful seasonal pattern suggesting entry around mid-November. As mentioned earlier, this is the preceding trade to Trade #8 for CPZ. The trade is always entered long, and has been profitable in 10 out of 11 years entered since 1971. One year showed no entry. This trade has a value for the Trader's Advantage of 0.90, and has earned a rank order of 16 out of 18 in the portfolio.

HISTORICAL RECORD:

1. Total Years Observed: 12.
   Profit Years: 10
   Loss Years: 1
   No Trade Years: 1
2. % Profitable Years: 91%
3. % Loss Years: 9%
4. Average Profit/Year: $2716 (basis 80¢ CPN)
5. Average Loss/Year: $ – 1480
6. **Trader's Advantage: 0.90**
7. (Average Annual Trade Profits)/Margin Required: 1.56

JULY COPPER

12 YEARS

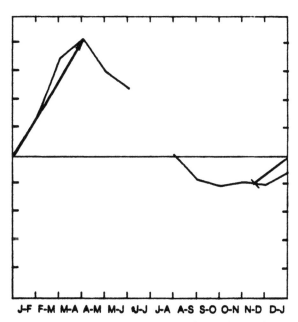

J-F F-M M-A A-M M-J U-J J-A A-S S-O O-N N-D D-J

Reprinted from *"Profits Through Seasonal Trading"* by Jack Gruschow and Courtney Smith
Courtesy of J. Wiley and Sons, publisher.

Rules For Trade #18
JULY COPPER (CPN)

1. After 11/15, buy long July Copper on any close that breaks a 5-week trendline.

2. After 11/1, buy any new season high close in CPN.

3. If long, place a protective stop at the season lows for the CPN contract.

4. If stopped out via (3), buy long CPN again via (1) or (2), if signaled.

5. Close profitable positions via a close that breaks a 5-week trendline.

6. Do not enter any long CPN position after 3/1.

7. Close the trade on 7/1 if still open.

Historical Results For Trade #18
JULY COPPER (CPN)

Margin: $1500

CY	ENTRY DATE	RULE #	L/S	PRICE	EXIT DATE	RULE #	PRICE	P/L (points)		P/L (%)	$ P/L (basis 80¢ CPN)
1971	12/11/70	1	L	49.20	1/ 6/71	3	46.30	− 290 }	+ 560	+ 11.4	+ 2115
	1/30/71	1	L	47.50	4/26/71	5	56.00	+ 850 }			
1972	12/ 2/71	1	L	47.50	1/19/72	5	49.60	+ 210		+ 4.4	+ 800
1973	11/30/72	1	L	50.00	3/27/73	5	64.20	+ 1420		+ 28.4	+ 5600
1974	11/ 9/73	2	L	82.00	4/ 8/74	5	115.00	+ 3300		+ 40.2	+ 7960
1975	12/26/74	1	L	58.00	12/31/74	3	56.00	− 200 }	+ 225	+ 3.8	+ 620
	1/27/75	1	L	56.00	4/ 4/75	5	60.25	+ 425 }			
1976	12/17/75	1	L	56.70	3/29/76	5	62.50	+ 580		+ 10.2	+ 1960
1977	12/ 9/76	1	L	61.20	2/ 9/77	5	67.30	+ 610		+ 10.0	+ 1915
1978	12/ 8/77	1	L	60.80	1/10/78	5	61.60	+ 80		+ 1.3	+ 160
1979	1/18/79	2	L	76.50	3/ 8/79	5	89.00	+ 1250		+ 16.4	+ 3200
1980	1/16/80	2	L	120.00	2/19/80	5	137.50	+ 1750		+ 14.6	+ 2835
1981	N.T.	—	—	—	—	—	—	—		—	No Trade
1982	12/ 2/81	1	L	81.50	12/10/81	3	75.80	− 570		− 7.0	− 1480
1983	12/ 7/82	1	L	71.50	2/28/83	5	76.70	+ 520		+ 7.3	+ 1380

All P/L Results Include Commission Costs

CHAPTER VII

PORTFOLIO
TRADING RESULTS

This chapter will be used to demonstrate the power of portfolio trading for the 18 seasonal trades which were detailed in Chapter VI. In selecting those 18 trades I aimed to maximize their contribution to the portfolio in the following two ways:

1. As many different markets as possible were used, giving the trader a good chance to capitalize on several really big, profitable moves each year.

2. The selected trades were spread across the various months of the

year, making the total margin required at any one time relatively even throughout the year.

Each of the 18 trades (along with twelve additional trades discussed in Chapter VIII) have been developed by me over the past 15 years of trading these many markets. As you might expect, different numbers of contracts were used for the various trades. There is a range of from 1 to 4 contracts traded per trade, making for an initial margin requirement for most trades of between $1500 and $2000. (The maximum initial margin being $3500 for the gold trades, if you choose to trade the 100 oz. contract).

The portfolio which I have studied most extensively for the previously listed 18 trades consists of the following:

Trade #	Commodity	# Of Contracts	Total Margin Req'd
1	PBN	1	$ 2,000
2	CZ/WZ	3	$ 1,800
3	SN/SX	3	$ 1,950
4	LHM	2	$ 1,600
5	GOM	1-Mid-Am or, 1-Comex	$ 1,500 or, $ 3,500
6	PWN	2	$ 1,500
7	CZ	4	$ 2,000
8	CPZ	1	$ 1,500
9	1½LHN/PBN	1	$ 2,000
10	BOZ	2	$ 2,000
11	CCZ	1	$ 2,000
12	OZ	4	$ 2,000
13	WZ	2	$ 2,000
14	SX	1	$ 1,750
15	GOM	1-Comex	$ 3,500
16	CTN	1	$ 2,000
17	PBG	1	$ 2,000
18	CPN	1	$ 1,500

The following four figures (Figs. 10 - 13) show the results for the portfolio for four of the past twelve years. The four years displayed (1973, 1976, 1979, and 1982) include the best year (1973), and one of the poorest years (1982). The years 1976 (Profits = $43,725) and 1979 (Profits = $43,330) are included as being representative of average profit results for a year. You will note that the results are based on only minimal use of portfolio profits as they accrued. Specifically, profits from closed trades were available for margin purposes, but profits from open trades were not. Also, the number of contracts traded later in the year was not increased beyond the original plan. The number of "later in the year" contracts obviously could have been increased through use of the large profits already made by that time, if so desired. However, increasing the number of contracts traded would violate the basic portfolio trading strategy, and is better left to more adventuresome traders.

I have summarized in Table 4 (on page 115) the average % profit for each year. These numbers are based on an investment of 2 times the maximum value of "margin required minus closed profits" for anytime during that year. This investment strategy is consistent with the "probability of ruin" concept detailed in Chapter III. There we demonstrated that as long as the portfolio possesses trades which have a Trader's Advantage greater than 0.80 and we operate with an investment policy of using up to 50% of the portfolio assets for margin purposes at any one time, the probability of ruin will be less than 4%.

Since the value of the Trader's Advantage for each of the trades in the portfolio is larger than 0.90, our investment strategy seems more than conservative. This statement holds true, I believe, even after allowing for inevitable bad trade executions, and for possible "statistical degradation" of profit performance of the various trades ("statistical degradation" was discussed when we considered the somewhat small sample sizes employed in the original determination of the value of the Trader's Advantage for each trade). Furthermore, inspection of the details of Figures 10 - 13 reveals that the portfolio was never in danger of a margin call when utilizing this strategy of maintaining equity in the account of at least 2 times the maximum margin required. For instance, in 1973, an initial margin requirement of $8000 necessitated a required investment of $16,000 for the portfolio. End of year profits that year were $132,415, yielding a return on initial investment of $828%. This calculation obviously does not

107

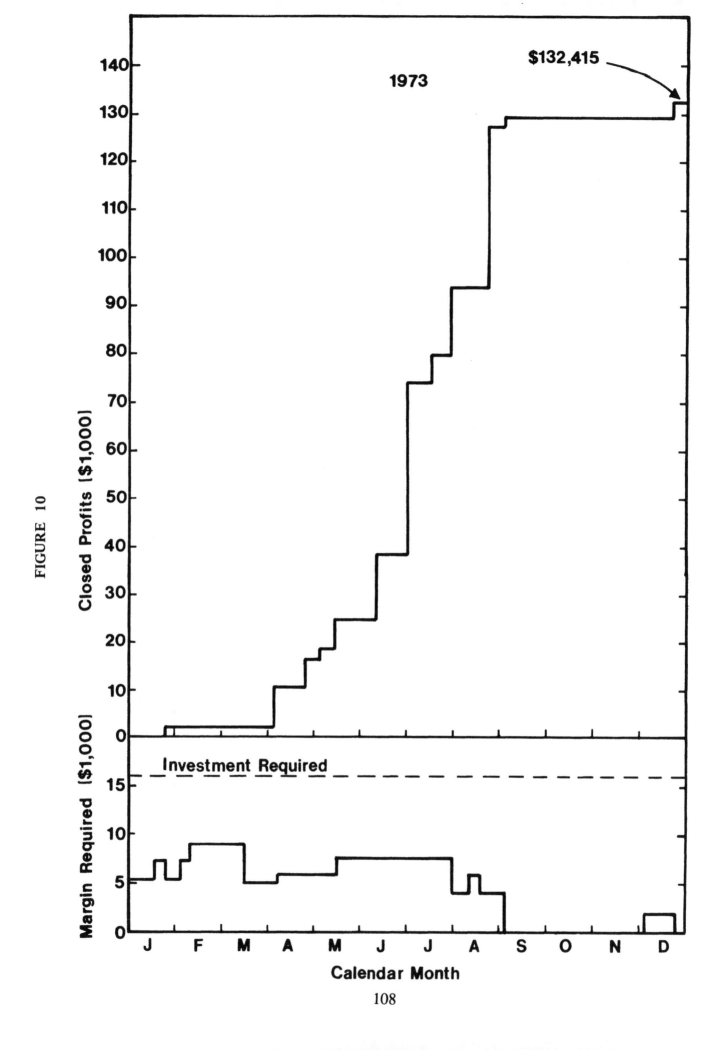

FIGURE 10

108

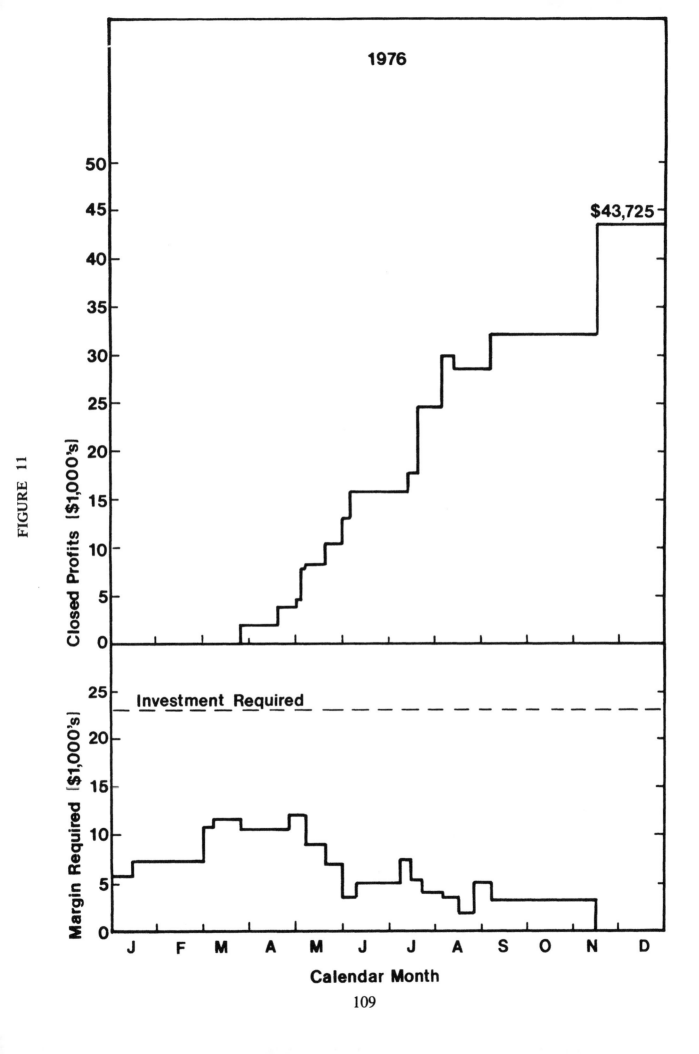

FIGURE 11

109

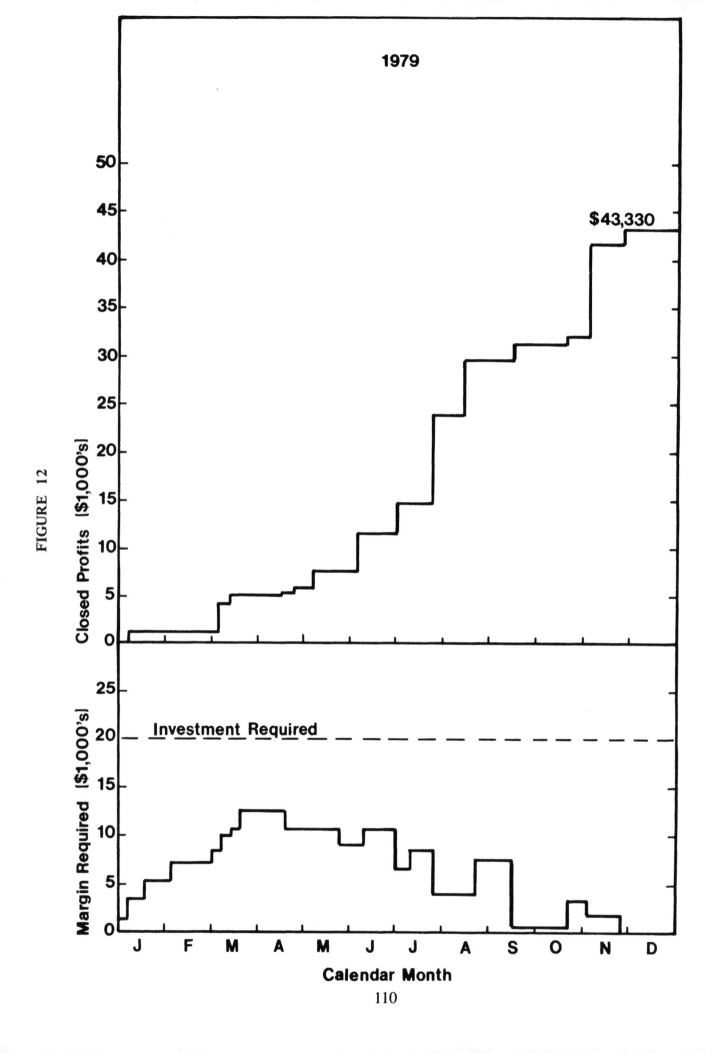

FIGURE 12

110

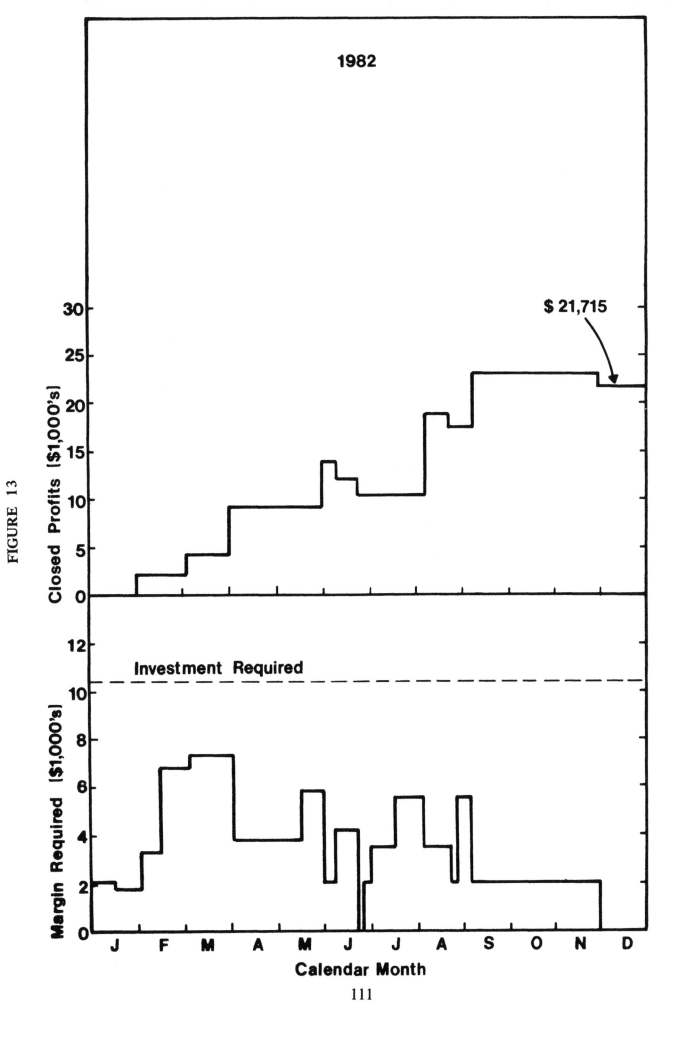

FIGURE 13

111

take into account the fact that large profits were accrued during the year and, subsequently, that the initial investment of $16,000 was not required beyond about March 15th.

To more fully demonstrate the importance of a diversified portfolio, I have listed here in Table 3 the two trades that made the most money in each year of trading.

TABLE 3
The Two Best Trades For Each Year

CY	Best Trade		Second Best Trade	
1971	#10 :BOZ	: $ 6,120	#12 :OZ	: $ 3,940
1972	#13 :WZ	: $12,540	#17 :PBG	: $ 8,090
1973	# 3 :SN/SX	: $35,010	#13 :WZ	: $21,090
1974	# 7 :CZ	: $21,320	#10 :BOZ	: $14,280
1975	# 7 :CZ	: $ 9,720	#11 :CCZ	: $ 5,910
1976	#15 :GOZ	: $11,430	#10 :BOZ	: $ 7,010
1977	# 3 :SN/SX	: $22,710	#12 :OZ	: $ 9,160
1978	# 3 :SN/SX	: $10,410	# 9 :LHN/PBN:	$ 9,370
1979	#15 :GOZ	: $ 9,670	# 7 :CZ	: $ 9,240
1980	# 7 :CZ	: $ 6,680	# 2 :CZ/WZ	: $ 4,830
1981	# 2 :CZ/WZ:	$ 9,780	#11 :CCZ	: $ 5,910
1982	#15 :GOZ	: $ 5,680	# 2 :CZ/WZ	: $ 4,830
	Average:	$13,420	Average:	$ 8,640

As you can see, 10 of the 18 trades in the portfolio are listed at least once in this table of the "two best trades" for each year. This clearly demonstrates the power and importance of portfolio diversification even in relatively small portfolios such as this one.

A second important point can be derived from this table. First notice that, on average, the "two best trades" made over $22,000 each year. This number, when compared with the average value for profits from the entire portfolio of $53,800 (see Table 4), means that the "two best trades" averaged over 40% of the profits for the entire portfolio. The point to be

112

made here is that, although diversification is important, you must not try to "pick and choose" your favorite trades for a particular year. By doing so, you may easily miss the best trades for the year and come away with smaller profits than were really available to you.

Another popular way to evaluate portfolio performance is through the concept of "portfolio drawdown." This is a day-by-day bookkeeping exercise which keeps track of the precise value of the portfolio equity in terms of the open trades as well as the closed trades. In tracking the value of the portfolio equity, "portfolio drawdown" thereby compares equity with margin requirements on a daily basis. I do not believe such close scrutiny is necessary to evaluate the model portfolio performance, particularly since this investment strategy is so conservative. However, to satisfy the non-believers, I have performed a "drawdown" analysis for the year 1982. I selected 1982 because it is the year with the poorest performance in terms of the percentage of losing trades for the year. The results are displayed in Figure 14. I used a starting portfolio equity level of $10,500. This is the same level as was used in the analysis of the yearly trading results displayed in Figure 13. In fact, Figure 14 is nearly a duplicate of Figure 13. The only difference between the two figures is the addition of a dashed line representing the moving value of the total portfolio equity in Figure 13. As you can see, by beginning the year with an investment of $10,500, portfolio drawdown never became an issue as far as day-to-day margin requirements were concerned. In fact, after about mid-March, we could have withdrawn $10,000 from the account and never have needed it for margin purposes.

Finally, in Table 4, I have provided a Summary of Results for the portfolio for the twelve years from 1971 to 1982. It lists: (1) the number of profitable years, loss years, and "no trade" years for each trade; (2) the investment required for each year; (3) the total profits for the year; and (4) the % return on investment. For additional conservativism, I have required at least $10,000 in investment equity each year. In two of the years observed, however, it would have been possible to get by with less than $10,000 initial equity and still not have exceeded having 50% of the funds committed at any one time.

113

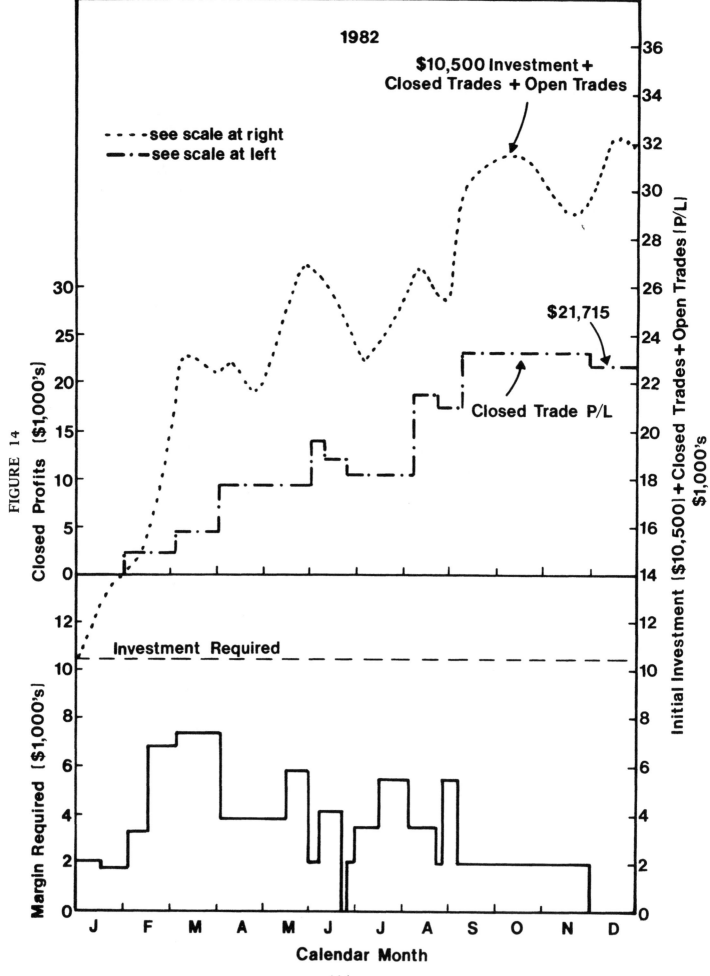

FIGURE 14

114

TABLE 4
Summary of Results For 18 Best Trades

CY	P/L/N.T.	Investment Required	Profits	% Return on Investment
1971	13/ 1/4	$10,000	$ 30,275	+ 303%
1972	14/ 2/2	$10,000	$ 49,615	+ 496%
1973	15/ 1/2	$16,000	$132,415	+ 828%
1974	15/ 1/2	$10,000	$ 74,980	+ 750%
1975	15/ 0/3	$18,000	$ 40,650	+ 226%
1976	14/ 1/3	$23,000	$ 43,725	+ 190%
1977	18/ 0/0	$18,000	$ 78,990	+ 439%
1978	16/ 1/1	$20,000	$ 59,875	+ 299%
1979	17/ 0/1	$20,000	$ 43,330	+ 217%
1980	16/ 0/2	$12,000	$ 40,330	+ 336%
1981	11/ 1/6	$14,500	$ 29,785	+ 205%
1982	8/ 6/4	$10,500	$ 21,715	+ 207%
		Average:	$ 53,807	+ 375%

CHAPTER VIII

TWELVE SEASONAL TRADES FOR FUTURE USE

The twelve trades detailed in this chapter are intended to supplement those in Chapter VI. They can either be used as part of a larger portfolio, or perhaps, to satisfy some personal trading interest of the investor. Some of these trades have better trading results than the primary portfolio trades in Chapter VI, and some have worse.

The results of the individual trades are presented in the following pages using the same format that was used in Chapter VI. In Table 5, on the following page, is a compilation of the important results for all of these trades.

TABLE 5
Summary of Results For 12 Trades For Future Use

Rank Order	Trade	Trade #	"A"	Avg. Profit/ Margin Req'd	P/L/N.T.
1	SX/SN	4A	1.0	8.61	5/0/7
2	CCU	1A	1.0	1.93	12/0/0
3	LHZ	6A	1.0	1.76	5/0/7
4	PBG	8A	1.0	1.04	12/0/0
5	SMZ/SMU	5A	0.97	3.16	8/3/1
6	WK	10A	0.97	1.55	6/1/5
7	LHQ	2A	0.96	1.73	10/2/0
8	CN	11A	0.91	2.20	4/1/7
9	SX	7A	0.87	3.36	10/2/0
10	PWK	12A	0.87	2.10	10/2/0
11	LCQ	3A	0.66	1.38	9/3/0
12	WH	9A	0.49	0.68	10/2/0
		Average:	0.89	2.46	

Trade #1A
SEPTEMBER COCOA (CCU)

This trade in September Cocoa is designed to take advantage of the up-move which often begins in the Winter and extends through most of the year for Cocoa. Trade #11 in CCZ (presented earlier), carries the trade from mid-year into early Fall. This trade in CCU is a highly profitable trade in spite of the fact that it has been reversed in 4 of the past 12 years. Some of the biggest profits were, in fact, made on those contra-seasonal moves. Note also that the trade has returned profits every year since 1971.

HISTORICAL RECORD:
1. Total Years Observed: 12
   Profit Years: 12
   Loss Years: 0
   No Trade Years: 0
2. % Profitable Years: 100%
3. % Loss Years: 0
4. Average Profit/Year: $3850 (basis $2000 CCU)
5. Average Loss/Year: $ 0
6. **Trader's Advantage: 1.0**
7. (Average Annual Trade Profits)/Margin Required: 1.93

SEPTEMBER COCOA

11 YEARS

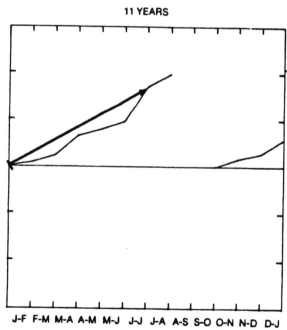

J-F F-M M-A A-M M-J J-J J-A A-S S-O O-N N-D D-J

Reprinted from *"Profits Through Seasonal Trading"* by Jack Gruschow and Courtney Smith
Courtesy of J. Wiley and Sons, publisher.

Rules For Trade #1A
SEPTEMBER COCOA (CCU)

1. After 5 days of trading in January, sell short September Cocoa on a 5-wk-D signal (close only); or, if it occurs first, buy long CCU on a 5-wk-D signal (close only).

2. Protect the position entered via (1) with a reverse stop (close only) placed at the highs (if short) or lows (if long) of trading for the 5-weeks prior to entry.

3. After prices move 4% in the direction of the trade (intraday), move the stop to the original 5-wk-D level used for entry in (1).

4. If reversed via (3), place a new reverse stop at the prior 6-weeks highs (if short), or lows (if long).

5. After prices move at least 10% in the direction of the trade, close on a 8-wk trendline signal (close only).

6. After prices move at least 15% in the direction of the trade, close on a 6-wk trendline signal (close only).

7. Do not use rules (5), (6), or (8) within 3 weeks of entry into a trade.

8. After prices move 25% in the direction of the trade (intraday), close on a 1HC3 signal (if short), or on a 1LC3 signal (if long).

9. After prices move 30% in the direction of the trade (intraday), close on the first higher close than the prior day's close (if short), or on the first lower close than the prior day's close (if long).

10. If short, after 4/8, close on a 12TL signal (close only).

11. If long, after 6/15, and if prices have moved at least 10% in the direction of the trade, close on a 6 TL signal (close only).

Historical Results For Trade #1A
SEPTEMBER COCOA (CCU)

Margin: $2000

CY	ENTRY DATE	RULE #	L/S	PRICE	EXIT DATE	RULE #	PRICE	P/L (points)			P/L (%)	$ P/L (basis $2000 CCU)
1971	1/ 7/71	1	S	28.35	3/14	5	24.75	+ 360			+ 12.7	+ 2460
1972	1/10/72	1	L	24.50	4/10	5	26.10	+ 160			+ 6.5	+ 1200
1973	1/20/73	1	S	30.80	2/23	2	35.00	− 420 }	+	820	+ 26.6	+ 5120
	2/23/73	2	L	35.00	5/13	9	47.40	+1240 }				
1974	2/ 7/74	1	L	53.70	9/ 4	9	74.30	+2060			+ 38.4	+ 7570
1975	1/10/75	1	L	61.00	2/24	3	59.00	− 200 }	+1000		+ 16.4	+ 3090
	2/24/75	3	S	59.00	5/ 9	8	47.00	+1200 }				
1976	1/ 7/76	1	L	61.75	2/27	9	79.25	+1550			+ 25.1	+ 4920
1977	1/ 8/77	1	L	131.50	2/10	9	167.00	+3550			+ 27.0	+ 5300
1978	1/17/78	1	S	122.00	2/27	3	127.50	− 550 }	+2000		+ 16.4	+ 3080
	2/27/78	3	L	127.50	4/ 3	8	153.00	+2550 }				
1979	1/12/79	1	S	167.70	4/12	6	145.00	+2270			+ 13.5	+ 2610
1980	2/ 8/80	1	L	148.00	3/13	2	135.00	−1300 }	+1900		+ 12.8	+ 2400
	3/13/80	2	S	135.00	7/ 2	8	103.00	+3200 }				
1981	2/ 2/81	1	S	2030.00	6/22	9	1450.00	+ 580			+ 28.6	+ 5620
1982	3/ 1/82	1	S	1985.00	4/23	6	1685.00	+ 300			+ 15.1	+ 2930

All P/L Results Include Commission Costs

121

Trade #2A
AUGUST LIVE HOGS (LHQ)

This trade in August Live Hogs, like Trade #4 for June Hogs, is designed to take advantage of the Spring bull move in hogs. It is not quite as reliable as Trade #4, but equally profitable for most years. In fact, the average profit from this trade is slightly larger than that from the LHM trade. However, it is not quite as reliable as it has suffered net losses in 2 of the 12 years observed.

HISTORICAL RECORD:

1. Total Years Observed: 12
        Profit Years: 10
        Loss Years: 2
        No Trade Years: 0
2. % Profitable Years: 83%
3. % Loss Years: 17%
4. Average Profit/Year: $1707 (basis $50.00 LHQ)
5. Average Loss/Year: $ – 173
6. **Trader's Advantage: 0.96**
7. (Average Annual Trade Profits)/Margin Required: 1.73

AUGUST HOGS

8 YEARS

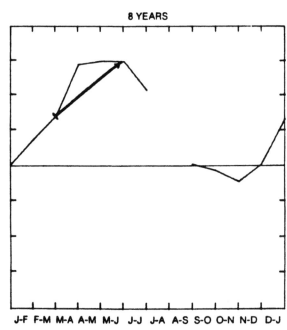

J-F F-M M-A A-M M-J J-J J-A A-S S-O O-N N-D D-J

Reprinted from *"Profits Through Seasonal Trading"* by Jack Gruschow and Courtney Smith
Courtesy of J. Wiley and Sons, publisher.

122

Rules For Trade #2A
AUGUST LIVE HOGS (LHQ)

1. On or after the last trading day in February, buy long August Hogs on a 5½-wk trendline signal (close only).

2. On or after the last trading day in February, buy long August Hogs on a new season high close signal.

3. After the last trading day in February, sell short August Hogs on any close lower than the lows recorded from December 1 to February 28.

4. Use rules (5) - (8) to close, or *reverse* the position (if a loss is recorded) taken by rules (1) - (3); also, use this rule for positions taken via rules (5) - (8).

5. Close long positions, or reverse to short if a loss trade, on any 5-wk TL signal.

6. Close long positions on any 8-wk TL signal (intraday).

7. Close short positions, or reverse to long if a loss trade, on any 5-wk TL signal (close only).

8. Close short positions on any 8-wk TL signal (intraday).

Historical Results For Trade #2A
AUGUST LIVE HOGS (LHQ)

Margin: $800

CY	ENTRY DATE	RULE #	L/S	PRICE	EXIT DATE	RULE #	PRICE	P/L (points)		P/L (%)	$ P/L (basis $50.00 LHQ)
1971	3/10/71	1	L	21.45	4/15	5	22.25	+ 80		+ 3.7	+ 500
1972	3/ 7/72	1	L	26.05	5/17	6	28.00	+ 195		+ 7.6	+ 1085
1973	3/ 7/73	2	L	36.00	6/ 7	5	39.50	+ 350		+ 9.7	+ 1400
1974	7/14/74	3	S	39.50	6/14	6	25.00	+1450		+36.7	+ 5440
1975	3/14/75	1	L	42.80	4/30	5, 6	47.20	+ 440		+10.3	+ 1480
1976	4/ 2/76	1	L	44.50	5/ 5	5	46.50	+ 200		+ 4.5	+ 615
1977	3/11/77	2	L	38.70	5/12	5	44.30	+ 560		+14.5	+ 2110
1978	3/ 7/78	2	L	46.20	6/ 1	6	52.80	+ 660		+14.3	+ 2080
1979	4/ 9/79	1	L	47.50	5/ 9	3	44.20	- 330 }	+140	+ 2.9	+ 315
	5/ 9/79	3	S	44.20	6/13	7	39.50	+ 470 }			
1980	3/ 3/80	1	L	42.80	3/24	3	38.80	- 400 }	+ 30	+ 0.7	- 15
	3/24/80	3	S	38.80	6/ 9	7	34.50	+ 430 }			
1981	2/27/81	3	S	50.00	3/31	1	52.60	- 260 }	-100	- 2.0	- 330
	3/31/81	1	L	52.60	6/26	6	54.20	+ 160 }			
1982	3/ 9/82	2	L	52.95	5/20	6	60.40	+ 745		+14.1	+ 2045

All P/L Results Include
Commission Costs

124

Trade #3A
AUGUST LIVE CATTLE (LCQ)

As you can see from the figure below, the seasonal charts are strongly supportive of this trade in August Live Cattle. However, seasonal trades are notoriously tricky in the cattle market; they often turn on you at the most unexpected time. This is one of the few trades I have been able to develop for cattle that I am willing to recommend. It is one of only a few cattle trades to offer the added benefit of being seasonally supported.

HISTORICAL RECORD:

1. Total Years Observed: 12
    Profit Years: 9
    Loss Years: 3
    No Trade Years: 0
2. % Profitable Years: 75%
3. % Loss Years: 25%
4. Average Profit/Year: $2900 (basis $68.00 LCQ)
5. Average Loss/Year: $-1812
6. **Trader's Advantage: 0.66**
7. (Average Annual Trade Profits)/Margin Required: 1.38

AUGUST LIVE CATTLE

10 YEARS

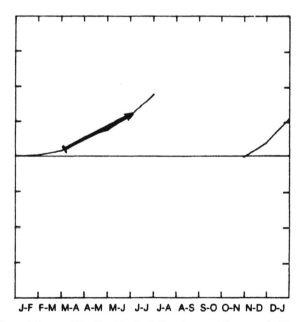

Reprinted from *"Profits Through Seasonal Trading"* by Jack Gruschow and Courtney Smith
Courtesy of J. Wiley and Sons, publisher.

125

Rules For Trade #3A
AUGUST LIVE CATTLE (LCQ)

1. Buy long August Live Cattle on the close of the first Friday in March.

2. Place a protective stop at the lows recorded between January 1 and entry date.

2a) If entry price is near the season low for the year, place the protective stop at the lows for the first two weeks of trading in March.

3. After 4/20, close the long LCQ trade on a 3-wk-D signal (close only).

4. If still open on the last trading day in May, close the trade on that day.

Historical Results For Trade #3A
AUGUST LIVE CATTLE (LCQ)

Margin: $1250

CY	ENTRY DATE	RULE #	L/S	PRICE	EXIT DATE	RULE #	PRICE	P/L (points)	P/L (%)	$ P/L (basis $68.00 LCQ)
1971	3/5/71	1	L	30.30	5/28	4	31.50	+ 120	+ 4.0	+ 1000
1972	3/3/72	1	L	32.90	5/31	4	36.00	+ 310	+ 9.4	+ 2490
1973	3/2/73	1	L	44.20	5/31	4	47.00	+ 280	+ 6.3	+ 1650
1974	3/1/74	1	L	49.20	4/29	2a	45.20	− 400	− 8.1	− 2285
1975	3/7/75	1	L	35.80	5/30	4	46.70	+ 1090	+ 30.4	+ 8205
1976	3/5/76	1	L	43.40	5/ 5	3	45.60	+ 220	+ 5.1	+ 1300
1977	3/4/77	1	L	41.95	5/ 9	3	43.00	+ 105	+ 2.5	+ 605
1978	3/3/78	1	L	46.90	5/31	4	58.90	+ 1200	+ 25.6	+ 6885
1979	3/2/79	1	L	68.20	5/ 7	3	72.60	+ 440	+ 6.5	+ 1680
1980	3/7/80	1	L	72.85	3/24	2	66.85	− 600	− 8.2	− 2315
1981	3/6/81	1	L	67.90	3/16	2a	66.00	− 190	− 3.0	− 835
1982	3/5/82	1	L	62.60	5/28	4	68.05	+ 545	+ 8.7	+ 2295

All P/L Results Include Commission Costs

Trade #4A
NOVEMBER SOYBEANS/ JULY SOYBEANS (SX/SN)

This spread trade of long November, short July soybeans is the follow-on trade to Trade #3 in SN/SX. Like Trade #3, this spread does not occur every year (it occurred in 5 out of the last 12 years). When it does occur, though, it can be hugely profitable. In fact, it is the most profitable trade detailed in the entire book, based on average return on margin. It is signaled for entry when the Spring strength in soybeans (if it occurs) breaks down. The trade takes advantage of the fact that new crop beans at this time of year weaken less than old crop beans, since there are still plenty of crop difficulties that can occur with the new crop.

HISTORICAL RECORD:

1. Total Years Observed: 12
      Profit Years: 5
      Loss Years: 0
      No Trade Years: 7
2. % Profitable Years: 100%
3. % Loss Years: 0
4. Average Profit/Year: $5600
5. Average Loss/Year: $ 0
6. **Trader's Advantage: 1.0**
7. (Average Annual Trade Profits)/Margin Required: 11.2

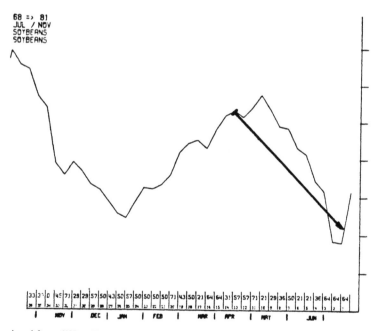

Reprinted from *"How To Profit From Seasonal Commodity Spreads"* by Jacob Bernstein
Courtesy of J. Wiley and Sons, publisher.

Rules For Trade #4A
NOVEMBER SOYBEANS/JULY SOYBEANS (SX/SN)

Keep a daily chart of the closing price difference of November Soybeans minus July Soybeans (SX/SN).

1. To enter this trade, require that the July Soybeans trend be up from January 1 to March 1.

2. After 3/20, enter the spread trade long SX/short SN on a 4-wk trendline signal from the July Soybeans daily bar chart (close only). This signal would require that the SN close *below* an *up-trending* 4-wk trendline.

3.a) Close the spread trade on 6/30 or via 3b.
   b) If the trend in the spread chart for SX/SN is firmly up going into 6/30, close the spread trade after 6/30 on the 1st day when the spread closes lower than the close of the prior day. Update this price on a daily basis until the trade is closed.

Historical Results For Trade #4A
NOVEMBER SOYBEANS/ JULY SOYBEANS (SX/SN)
Margin $650

CY	ENTRY DATE	PRICE	EXIT DATE	PRICE	P/L (points)	$ P/L
1971	N.T.	–	–	–	–	–
1972	4/27/72	– 33¾	6/30	– 24¼	+ 9½	+ 400
1973	6/29/73	– 407	7/10	– 170	+ 237	+ 11,790
1974	N.T.	–	–	–	–	–
1975	N.T.	–	–	–	–	–
1976	N.T.	–	–	–	–	–
1977	4/26/77	– 274	7/15	– 40	+ 234	+ 11,640
1978	3/29/78	– 104	6/30	– 54½	+ 49½	+ 2,400
1979	4/ 3/79	– 59	6/30	– 2½	+ 56½	+ 2,750
1980	N.T.	–	–	–	–	–
1981	N.T.	–	–	–	–	–
1982	N.T.	–	–	–	–	–

All P/L Results Include
Commission Costs

130

Trade #5A
DECEMBER SOYBEAN MEAL/ SEPTEMBER SOYBEAN MEAL
(SMZ/SMU)

This spread trade in new crop/old crop soybean meal is based on the same events that work for Trade #4A in soybeans. Although not quite as reliable or profitable as 4A, this spread is an active trade more often than is the bean spread trade.

HISTORICAL RECORD:

1. Total Years Observed: 12
    Profit Years: 8
    Loss Years: 3
    No Trade Years: 1
2. % Profitable Years: 73%
3. % Loss Years: 27%
4. Average Profit/Year: $2210
5. Average Loss/Year: − $93
6. **Trader's Advantage: 0.97**
7. (Average Annual Trade profits)/Margin Required: 3.16

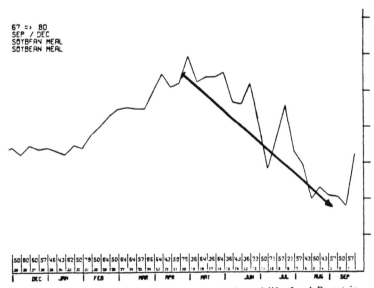

Reprinted from *"How To Profit From Seasonal Commodity Spreads"* by Jacob Bernstein Courtesy of J. Wiley and Sons, publisher.

131

Rules For Trade #5A
DECEMBER SOYBEAN MEAL/SEPTEMBER SOYBEAN MEAL
(SMZ/SMU)

1. After 4/14, enter the spread trade long December Soybean Meal/short September Soybean Meal on a 4TL or 4-wk-D sell signal obtained from the daily bar chart for the *July* Soybean Meal. This would require that the SMN close *below* the 4TL or the 4-wk-D level.

2. Close the spread trade anytime between 9/1 and 9/4.

Historical Results For Trade #5A
DECEMBER SOYBEAN MEAL/SEPTEMBER SOYBEAN MEAL
(SMZ/SMU)

Margin: $500

CY	ENTRY DATE	PRICE	EXIT DATE	PRICE	P/L (points)	$ P/L
1971	N.T.	—	—	—	—	
1972	4/21/72	− 950	9/ 4/72	− 300	+ 600	+ 520
1973	6/28/73	− 13,500	9/ 4/73	− 1,750	+ 11,750	+ 11,670
1974	4/20/74	+ 300	9/ 4/74	+ 1,000	+ 700	+ 620
1975	4/21/75	+ 400	9/ 4/75	+ 450	+ 50	− 30
1976	6/17/76	− 220	9/ 4/76	+ 320	+ 100	+ 20
1977	4/26/77	− 4,200	9/ 4/77	− 350	+ 3,850	+ 3,770
1978	4/24/78	− 150	9/ 4/78	+ 200	+ 350	+ 270
1979	4/12/79	− 450	9/ 4/79	+ 400	+ 850	+ 770
1980	5/16/80	+ 650	9/ 4/80	+ 780	+ 130	+ 50
1981	4/28/81	+ 650	9/ 4/81	+ 560	− 90	− 170
1982	5/25/82	+ 450	9/ 4/82	+ 450	0	− 80

All P/L Results Include Commission Costs

Trade #6A
DECEMBER LIVE HOGS (LHZ)

The seasonal pattern for this short trade in December Live Hogs does not appear to be very impressive. In fact, the trade is intended to be entered only in those years when hogs fail to remain strong through the summer. You will note that it was entered in only 5 of the last 12 years. The trade was very reliable, though, as it was profitable in each of the 5 years it was entered.

HISTORICAL RECORD:

1. Total Years Observed: 12
   Profit Years: 5
   Loss Years: 0
   No Trade Years: 7
2. % Profitable Years: 100%
3. % Loss Years: 0
4. Average Profit/Year: $1408 (basis $50.00 LHZ)
5. Average Loss/Year: $ 0
6. **Trader's Advantage: 1.0**
7. (Average Annual Trade Profits)/Margin Required: 1.76

DECEMBER HOGS

7 YEARS

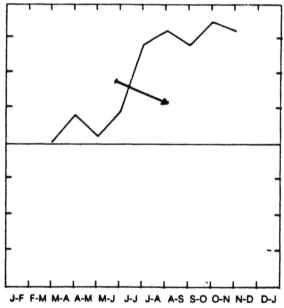

J-F F-M M-A A-M M-J J-J J-A A-S S-O O-N N-D D-J

Reprinted from *"Profits Through Seasonal Trading"* by Jack Gruschow and Courtney Smith
Courtesy of J. Wiley and Sons, publisher.

Rules For Trade #6A
DECEMBER LIVE HOGS (LHZ)

1. After 4/30, sell short December Live Hogs when LHZ closes lower than the lows recorded for the contract between 3/10 and 4/30.

2. Close the short position if the price of LHZ reaches a price 12% lower than the entry price; or, close on a 5½-wk trendline signal (close only).

3. Protect the short position with a stop at the season highs for the contract (close only).

4. Do not enter the trade after 11/1.

Historical Results For Trade #6A
DECEMBER LIVE HOGS (LHZ)

Margin: $800

CY	ENTRY DATE	RULE #	L/S	PRICE	EXIT DATE	RULE #	PRICE	P/L (points)	P/L (%)	$ P/L (basis $50.00 LHZ)
1971	6/18/71	1	S	21.40	8/18	2	19.25	+ 215	+ 10.0	+ 1435
1972	N.T.	–	–	–	–	–	–	–	–	–
1973	N.T.	–	–	–	–	–	–	–	–	–
1974	5/ 1/74	1	S	33.90	5/16	2	29.82	+ 408	+ 12.0	+ 1740
1975	N.T.	–	–	–	–	–	–	–	–	–
1976	7/27/76	1	S	38.50	9/23	2	33.88	+ 412	+ 12.0	+ 1735
1977	7/21/77	1	S	35.90	8/ 9	2	34.80	+ 110	+ 3.1	+ 395
1978	N.T.	–	–	–	–	–	–	–	–	–
1979	5/ 9/79	1	S	41.80	6/ 5	2	36.75	+ 505	+ 12.0	+ 1735
1980	N.T.	–	–	–	–	–	–	–	–	–
1981	N.T.	–	–	–	–	–	–	–	–	–
1982	N.T.	–	–	–	–	–	–	–	–	–

All P/L Results Include Commission Costs

136

Trade #7A
NOVEMBER SOYBEANS (SX)

This long trade in November Soybeans is one of my favorite seasonal trades. Driven largely by crop uncertainties, it has a beautiful seasonal chart (see below) and should be included in your trading plan whenever possible. Although it has shown reversal trades in 4 of the 12 years observed, this trade returns very large profits more often than not. If you want to trade soybeans on a regular basis, this is the trade to use.

HISTORICAL RECORD:

1. Total Years Observed: 12
   Profit Years: 10
   Loss Years: 2
   No Trade Years: 0
2. % Profitable Years: 83%
3. % Loss Years: 17%
4. Average Profit/Year: $7585 (basis $7.00 SX)
5. Average Loss/Year: − $2670
6. **Trader's Advantage: 0.87**
7. (Average Annual Trade Profits)/Margin Required: 3.36

NOVEMBER SOYBEANS

11 YEARS

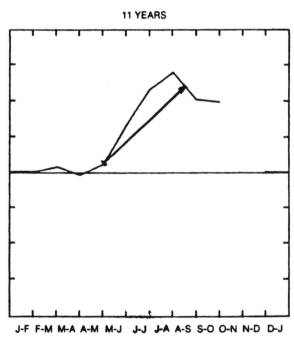

J-F F-M M-A A-M M-J J-J J-A A-S S-O O-N N-D D-J

Reprinted from *"Profits Through Seasonal Trading"* by Jack Gruschow and Courtney Smith
Courtesy of J. Wiley and Sons, publisher.

Rules For Trade #7A
NOVEMBER SOYBEANS (SX)

1. After 5/1, buy long November Soybeans on an 8-wk trendline signal (close only).

2. After 5/1, buy long November Soybeans on a new season high signal (close only).

3. After 5/1, sell short November Soybeans on a new season low signal (close only).

4. Close long positions entered via (1) or (2) using an 8-wk TL signal, if profitable.

4.a) If the trade entered via (1) or (2) is a loss trade, reverse the long position to a short position using an 8-wk TL signal.

5. If still open on 11/1, close the long or short position on that day.

6. Keep trading via Rules (1) - (4) until a trade is closed which makes a profit of at least 5¢ in SX.

Historical Results For Trade #7A
NOVEMBER SOYBEANS (SX)

Margin: $1750

CY	ENTRY DATE	RULE #	L/S	PRICE	DATE	RULE #	PRICE	P/L (points)	P/L (%)	$ P/L (basis $7.00 SX)
1971	5/21/71	1	L	2.91	7/26	4	3.31	+ 40	+ 13.5%	+ 4,755
1972	7/ 3/72	1	L	3.30	7/12	4a	3.19	− 11 }		
	7/12/72	4a	S	3.19	8/ 7	2	3.32	− 13 } − 18	− 6.0%	− 2,100
	8/ 7/72	2	L	3.32	10/ 9	4	3.38	+ 6 }		
1973	5/ 8/73	2	L	4.70	9/ 5	4	6.60	+190	+ 40.0%	+14,080
1974	5/28/74	1	L	5.60	10/28	4	7.90	+230	+ 41.1%	+14,475
1975	6/18/75	1	L	4.90	8/25	4	6.15	+125	+ 25.5%	+ 8,860
1976	5/ 7/76	1	L	5.20	7/19	4	7.05	+185	+ 35.6%	+12,400
1977	6/ 3/77	2	L	7.80	6/13	4a	7.10	− 70 } +120	+ 15.4%	+ 5,270
	6/13/77	4a	S	7.10	8/24	4	5.20	+190 }		
1978	5/25/78	2	L	6.48	7/ 3	4a	6.10	− 38		
	7/ 3/78	4a	S	6.10	7/27	1	6.09	+ 1 } + 54	+ 8.3%	+ 2,720
	7/27/78	1	L	6.09	11/ 1	5	7.00	+ 91 }		
1979	5/ 3/79	2	L	7.21	7/23	4	7.45	+ 24	+ 3.3%	+ 1,100
1980	5/ 8/80	1	L	6.62	9/26	4	8.16	+154	+ 23.3%	+ 8,075
1981	6/ 5/81	3	S	7.44	7/ 6	1	7.67	− 23 }		
	7/ 6/81	1	L	7.67	8/13	3	6.95	− 72 } − 65	− 8.7%	− 3,240
	8/13/81	3	S	6.95	10/ 5	4	6.65	+ 30 }		
1982	7/ 2/82	3	S	6.18	10/13	1	5.44	+ 74	+ 11.9%	+ 4,100

All P/L Results Include Commission Costs

139

Trade #8A
FEBRUARY PORK BELLIES (PBG)

Here's another belly trade that is remarkably reliable. It seeks to capitalize on the tendency for February Pork Bellies to weaken in late summer, a reliable seasonal pattern. The perfect record for returning profits over the past 12 years speaks for itself, even though the trade was reversed to long in 4 of those years. It's hard to argue with a trade that doubles your money in one to two months, year after year.

HISTORICAL RECORD:

1. Total Years Observed: 12
        Profit Years: 12
        Loss Years: 0
        No Trade Years: 0
2. % Profitable Years: 100%
3. % Loss Years: 0
4. Average Profit/Year: $2085 (basis 70¢ PBG)
5. Average Loss/Year: $ 0
6. **Trader's Advantage: 1.0**
7. (Average Annual Trade Profits)/Margin Required: 1.04

FEBRUARY PORK BELLIES

10 YEARS

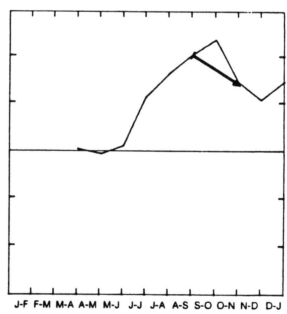

Reprinted from *"Profits Through Seasonal Trading"* by Jack Gruschow and Courtney Smith Courtesy of J. Wiley and Sons, publisher.

Rules For Trade #8A
FEBRUARY PORK BELLIES (PBG)

1. After 8/15, sell short February Pork Bellies on a 4-wk TL signal (close only).

2. Close the short PBG position via a 4-wk TL signal (close only). If this is a loss trade, reverse to being long *two* contracts of PBG for each original short contract. Hold these long contracts until the total profits from the long contracts equals 2-times the losses from the short trade.

3. If the short trade is open on 11/1, close the trade on the first close higher than the prior 3 closes (1HC3 signal). Update this price on a daily basis until the trade is closed.

141

Historical Results For Trade#8A
FEBRUARY PORK BELLIES (PBG)

Margin: $2,000

CY	ENTRY DATE	RULE #	L/S	PRICE	EXIT DATE	RULE #	PRICE	P/L (points)	P/L (%)	$ P/L (basis 70¢ PBG)
1971	10/15/71	1	S	31.80	11/ 5	2a	31.00	+ 80	+ 2.5%	+ 565
1972	9/21/72	1	S	47.00	10/30	2	47.00	+ 0 } + 100	+ 2.1%	+ 320
	10/30/72	2	L-2	47.00	10/31	2	47.50	+ 100 }		
1973	8/23/73	1	S	80.00	9/26	2	63.50	+ 1650	+ 20.6%	+ 5400
1974	10/14/74	1	S	68.00	11/ 8	2a	61.00	+ 700	+ 10.3%	+ 2660
1975	10/ 8/75	1	S	100.50	11/ 5	2a	83.00	+ 1750	+ 17.4%	+ 4550
1976	9/13/76	1	S	57.00	11/ 3	2a	48.00	+ 900	+ 15.8%	+ 4120
1977	9/12/77	1	S	49.20	10/25	2	49.00	+ 20	+ 0.4%	+ 30
1978	9/13/78	1	S	58.20	9/19	2	62.20	- 400 } + 400	+ 6.9%	+ 1590
	9/24/79	2	L-2	62.20	9/23	2	66.20	+ 800 }		
1979	7/24/79	1	S	44.80	10/22	2	43.90	+ 90	+ 2.0%	+ 455
1980	8/19/80	1	S	60.20	9/ 8	2	66.20	- 600 } + 600	+ 10.0%	+ 2410
	9/ 8/80	2	L-2	66.20	9/22	2	72.20	+ 1200 }		
1981	8/25/81	1	S	66.60	10/16	2	65.00	- 160 } + 160	+ 3.0%	+ 560
	10/16/81	2	L-2	65.00	10/19	2	66.80	+ 320 }		
1982	9/10/82	1	S	87.20	11/ 5	2a	79.20	+ 800	+ 9.2%	+ 2360

All P/L Results Include
Commission Costs

Trade #9A
MARCH WHEAT (WH)

This is a highly reliable trade, showing profits in 10 out of the past 12 years. Its major weakness is that it is inclined to yield large losses whenever it fails. This drawback should not really be surpirising, as the seasonal chart below doesn't offer much reassurance that the recommended long position in wheat will work very well. However, for modest profits from a Fall trade in wheat, this trade should not be neglected.

HISTORICAL RECORD:

1. Total Years Observed: 12
     Profit Years: 10
     Loss Years: 2
     No Trade Years: 0
2. % Profitable Years: 83%
3. % Loss Years: 17%
4. Average Profit/Year: $1170 (basis $3.80 WH)
5. Average Loss/Year: − $2088
6. **Trader's Advantage: 0.49**
7. (Average Annual Trade Profits)/Margin Required: 0.68

CHI MARCH WHEAT

11 YEARS

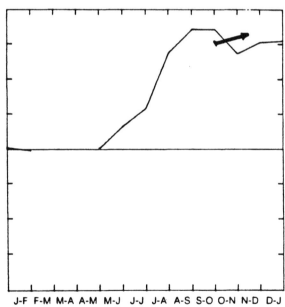

J-F F-M M-A A-M M-J J-J J-A A-S S-O O-N N-D D-J

Reprinted from *"Profits Through Seasonal Trading"* by Jack Gruschow and Courtney Smith Courtesy of J. Wiley and Sons, publisher.

Rules For Trade #9A
MARCH WHEAT (WH)

1. Buy long March Wheat on:
    (a) a 4-wk-D signal after the first trading week in September; or,
    (b) the close of the 2nd trading day in October.

2. Take profits on the long WH position via:
    (a) a 30¢ upmove in WH if the purchase price was in excess of $4.00/bu;
    (b) a 20¢ upmove in WH if the purchase price was in excess of $2.00/bu;
    (c) a 10¢ upmove in WH if the purchase price was lower than $2.00/bu;
    (d) if open on 12/31, sell the WH long position.

3. (a) Protect the long WH position with a reverse stop on a 5-wk-D signal (close only).
    (b) If reversed to short via (3a), hold until 11/15 and take profits that day; or
    (c) If no profit is available on 11/15, hold the short position and close when profits from that position equal 150% of the losses incurred in (3a).
    (d) Protect short positions entered via (3a) with a 4-wk-D stop (close only).

Historical Results For Trade #9A
MARCH WHEAT (WH)

Margin: $1000

CY	ENTRY DATE	RULE #	L/S	PRICE	EXIT DATE	RULE #	PRICE	P/L (points)	P/L (%)	$ P/L (basis $3.80 WH)
1971*	10/ 4/71	1b	L	1.47	12/ 9	2c	1.57	+ 10	+ 6.8	+ 1230
1972*	9/ 5/72	1a	L	2.06	11/ 5	2b	2.26	+ 20	+ 9.7	+ 1780
1973*	9/11/73	1a	L	4.88	9/21	2a	5.18	+ 30	+ 6.1	+ 1100
1974*	9/25/74	1a	L	4.75	9/30	2a	5.05	+ 30	+ 6.3	+ 1135
1975	10/ 2/75	1a	L	4.24	10/14	3a	4.18	− 6 } + 47	+ 11.0	+ 1960
	10/14/75	3a	S	4.18	11/15	3b	3.65	+ 53 }		
1976	10/ 4/76	1b	L	3.01	10/13	2a	3.21	+ 20	+ 6.6	+ 1190
1977	9/ 8/77	1a	L	2.48	9/13	2b	2.68	+ 20	+ 8.0	+ 1455
1978	9/ 7/78	1a	L	3.32	10/21	2b	3.52	+ 20	+ 6.0	+ 1075
1979	10/ 1/79	1a	L	4.81	10/26	3a	4.41	− 40 } − 59	− 12.3	− 2470
	10/26/79	3a	S	4.41	12/26	3d	4.60	− 19 }		
1980	9/19/80	1a	L	5.20	10/22	2a	5.00	+ 30	+ 5.7	+ 1030
1981	10/ 2/81	1b	L	4.52	10/18	3a	4.49	− 3 } + 16	+ 3.5	+ 535
	10/18/81	3a	S	4.49	12/ 7	3c	4.30	+ 19 }		
1982	10/ 4/82	1b	L	3.37	10/14	3a	3.29	− 8 } − 28	− 8.3	− 1705
	10/14/82	3a	S	3.29	11/ 5	2b	3.49	− 20 }		

All P/L Results Include Commission Costs

* WK used rather than WH for these trades.

145

Trade #10A
MAY WHEAT (WK)

This short trade in May Wheat does not occur every year. However, when it does occur, it is definitely worth your attention. I don't know of any fundamental factors to hold responsible for this seasonal pattern, but I do recognize a winning trade when I see one. In fact, the main events in the wheat market which lead to this trade opportunity are those associated with the seasonal pattern for wheat to go up from late summer into winter. When that pattern runs out of steam, this trade is the way to take advantage of the tired longs whose greed is about to be their undoing.

HISTORICAL RECORD:

1. Total Years Observed: 13
   Profit Years: 6
   Loss Years: 1
   No Trade Years: 6
2. % Profitable Years: 86%
3. % Loss Years: 14%
4. Average Profit/Year: $1835 (basis $3.80 WK)
5. Average Loss/Year: − $200
6. **Trader's Advantage: 0.97**
7. (Average Annual Trade Profits)/Margin Required: 1.55

CHI MAY WHEAT

11 YEARS

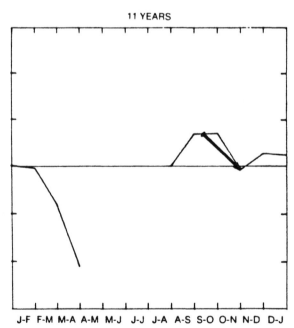

J-F F-M M-A A-M M-J J-J J-A A-S S-O O-N N-D D-J

Reprinted from *"Profits Through Seasonal Trading"* by Jack Gruschow and Courtney Smith
Courtesy of J. Wiley and Sons, publisher.

Rules For Trade #10A
MAY WHEAT (WK)

1. After 9/30 and before 1/5, sell short May Wheat on a close below the daily lows recorded in September.

2. Take profits when the price for WK declines to 90% of the entry price; or, close the short position on a 5-wk TL signal (close only).

Historical Results For Trade #10A
MAY WHEAT (WK)

Margin: $1000

CY	ENTRY RULE #	ENTRY DATE	L/S	PRICE	EXIT DATE	EXIT RULE #	PRICE	P/L (points)	P/L (%)	$ P/L (basis $3.80 WK)
1971	–	N.T.	–	–	–	–	–	–	–	–
1972	–	N.T.	–	–	–	–	–	–	–	–
1973	1	10/16/73	S	4.18	10/30	2	3.76	+ 42	+ 10.0	+ 1835
1974	1	1/ 7/75	S	4.20	1/20	2	3.78	+ 42	+ 10.0	+ 1835
1975	1	10/21/75	S	4.16	11/11	2	3.75	+ 41	+ 10.0	+ 1810
1976	1	10/26/76	S	2.97	11/11	2	2.67	+ 30	+ 10.0	+ 1855
1977	–	N.T.	–	–	–	–	–	–	–	–
1978	–	N.T.	–	–	–	–	–	–	–	–
1979	–	N.T.	–	–	–	–	–	–	–	–
1980	1	12/ 9/80	S	5.00	12/12	2	4.50	+ 50	+ 10.0	+ 1835
1981	1	11/24/81	S	4.45	12/25	2	4.00	+ 45	+ 10.0	+ 1835
1982	1	10/14/82	S	3.36	11/29	2	3.38	- 2	- .6	- 200

All P/L Results Include
Commission Costs

148

Trade #11A
JULY CORN (CN)

This short trade in July Corn is similar to #10A in May Wheat. It doesn't occur every year, but when it does, you can quickly take 200% profits out of the market. The seasonal chart is highly supportive of the trade, so you can go with the trade with great confidence.

HISTORICAL RECORD:

1. Total Years Observed: 12
   Profit Years: 4
   Loss Years: 1
   No Trade Years: 7
2. % Profitable Years: 80%
3. % Loss Years: 20%
4. Average Profit/Year: $1440 (basis $3.00 CN)
5. Average Loss/Year: −$260
6. **Trader's Advantage: 0.91**
7. (Average Annual Trade Profits)/Margin Required: 2.20

JULY CORN

11 YEARS

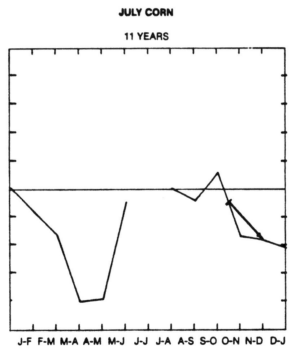

J-F F-M M-A A-M M-J J-J J-A A-S S-O O-N N-D D-J

Reprinted from *"Profits Through Seasonal Trading"* by Jack Gruschow and Courtney Smith
Courtesy of J. Wiley and Sons, publisher.

Rules For Trade #11A
JULY CORN (CN)

1. After 10/20 and before 1/1, sell short July Corn if CN closes below the lows recorded during the period 9/1 - 10/20.

2. Close the short position when CN declines to 90% of the entry price; or, close the CN position on a 6-wk TL signal (close only).

Historical Results For Trade #11A
JULY CORN (CN)

Margin: $500

CY	ENTRY DATE	RULE #	L/S	PRICE	EXIT DATE	RULE #	PRICE	P/L (points)	P/L (%)	$ P/L (basis $3.00 CN)
1971	N.T.	–	–	–	–	–	–	–	–	–
1972	N.T.	–	–	–	–	–	–	–	–	–
1973	N.T.	–	–	–	–	–	–	–	–	–
1974	12/26/74	1	S	3.32	2/28	2	2.99	+ 33	+ 10.0	+ 1440
1975	10/21/75	1	S	2.96	12/15	2	2.66	+ 30	+ 10.0	+ 1440
1976	10/26/76	1	S	2.78	11/12	2	2.50	+ 28	+ 10.0	+ 1440
1977	N.T.	–	–	–	–	–	–	–	–	–
1978	N.T.	–	–	–	–	–	–	–	–	–
1979	N.T.	–	–	–	–	–	–	–	–	–
1980	N.T.	–	–	–	–	–	–	–	–	–
1981	11/16/81	1	S	3.15	12/10	2	2.83	+ 31	+ 10.0	+ 1440
1982	10/22/82	1	S	2.49	11/15	2	2.52	- 3	- 1.2	- 260

All P/L Results Include
Commission Costs

151

Trade #12A
MAY PLYWOOD (PWK)

Here's another trade to fill out your portfolio, using an often-neglected market. Being long May Plywood from early winter into early spring is a highly reliable trading proposition, and is based on fundamental events in inventory management of the building industry. This trade has returned profits 10 out of the past 12 years, and in so doing, returned profits of over 200% on margin in less than 3 months. You will note that recessions are bad for this trade. The years 1981 and 1982 have been the only two loss years recorded since I began tracking this market in 1971.

HISTORICAL RECORD:

1. Total Years Observed: 12
     Profit Years: 10
     Loss Years: 2
     No Trade Years: 0
2. % Profitable Years: 83%
3. % Loss Years: 17%
4. Average Profit/Year: $2037 (basis $200.00 PWK)
5. Average Loss/Year: −$732
6. **Trader's Advantage: 0.87**
7. (Average Annual Trade Profits)/Margin Required: 2.10

MAY PLYWOOD

7 YEARS

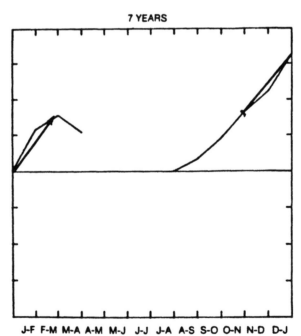

J-F F-M M-A A-M M-J J-J J-A A-S S-O O-N N-D D-J

Reprinted from *"Profits Through Seasonal Trading"* by Jack Gruschow and Courtney Smith
Courtesy of J. Wiley and Sons, publisher.

Rules For Trade #12A
MAY PLYWOOD (PWK)

1. After 10/30, buy long May Plywood on a 4-wk TL signal or on a season high signal (close only).

2. If unable to enter via (1) by 11/30, buy long PWK on the close on 11/30.

3. If entry occurs in November, during November use a protective stop at the lows of the prior 4-weeks of trading. After November, place a protective stop 1 tick lower than the November lows in PWK (for entries made via either (1) or (2)).

4. Close the long PWK position when the price goes up by 20% from the entry price. Or, after 2/6, close the trade on a 4-wk TL signal (close only). Close out the trade on whichever of these two conditions occurs first.

Historical Results For Trade #12A
MAY PLYWOOD (PWK)

Margin $750

CY	ENTRY DATE	RULE #	L/S	PRICE	EXIT DATE	RULE #	PRICE	P/L (points)	P/L (%)	$ P/L (basis $200.00 PWK)
1971	11/30/70	2	L	81.50	2/ 5/71	4	97.80	+ 1630	+ 20.0	+ 2975
1972	11/30/71	2	L	92.30	2/ 8/72	4	104.30	+ 1200	+ 13.0	+ 1935
1973	11/30/72	2	L	136.10	2/ 9/73	4	163.30	+ 2720	+ 20.0	+ 2975
1974	11/30/73	2	L	98.00	1/ 5/74	4	117.60	+ 1960	+ 20.0	+ 2975
1975	11/30/74	2	L	113.00	2/11/75	4	126.00	+ 1300	+ 11.5	+ 1710
1976	11/30/75	2	L	138.00	2/ 2/76	4	165.60	+ 2760	+ 20.0	+ 2975
1977	11/ 3/76	1	L	182.00	3/ 8/77	4	207.00	+ 2500	+ 13.8	+ 2030
1978	11/15/77	1	L	200.00	2/15/78	4	213.00	+ 1300	+ 6.5	+ 920
1979	11/24/78	1	L	199.00	2/22/79	4	214.00	+ 1500	+ 7.6	+ 1090
1980	11/ 1/79	1	L	186.00	2/15/80	4	196.50	+ 1050	+ 5.6	+ 785
1981	11/11/80	1	L	224.00	12/ 4/80	3	218.00	- 600 •	- 2.7	- 475
1982	11/12/81	1	L	205.50	1/ 5/82	3	193.00	- 1250	- 6.1	- 990

All P/L Results Include
Commission Costs

CHAPTER IX

CONCLUSIONS

I now want to summarize the most important ideas and information that have been presented in the prior eight chapters. The three primary elements of my method are: (1) utilize a *portfolio* of trades spread across several different markets and across the calendar year; (2) avoid financial ruin and make large profits by developing and utilizing "high reliability" trades; and (3) concentrate on *seasonal trades* to accomplish both (1) and (2).

To assist you in this plan, I provided a portfolio of 18 seasonal trades in Chapter VI, plus an additional 12 seasonal trades in Chapter VIII. The portfolio of 18 trades has a reliability of 93.3% and has yielded

155

approximately 375% profits per year for the past 12 years. The 30 trades outlined in Chapters VI and VIII have a combined reliability of 91%. In fact, 13 of the 30 trades have yielded profits *every year* since 1971, when traded according to the rules specified.

I speak from experience when I say that the most difficult task you will face in using these results in your own commodity trading will be to rigorously follow the rules and enter/exit when signaled. There will always be reasons not to act when and how you should. However, if you learn to trade by the rules, you will be surprised how well they will work. In addition, be careful not to take an unusually large position in one of the trades when you are particularly enthused about that trade's prospects. Those are the trades that fool you every time! Keep your portfolio balanced, be patient, and follow the rules. If you can do that, the only thing you will have to worry about will be paying your taxes.

APPENDICES

APPENDIX I
Listing Of All Trades By Market Type

MARKET TYPE	TRADE #	PAGE #	% PROFIT YEARS	AVG. ANNUAL PROFITS MARGIN REQ'D
Grains				
CN	11A	149	80%	2.20
CZ	7	68	75%	3.11
CZ/WZ	2	53	75%	1.92
SX	14	89	100%	1.50
SX	7A	137	83%	3.36
SN/SX	3	56	100%	6.06
SX/SN	4A	128	100%	8.61
BOZ	10	77	92%	2.16
SMZ/SMU	5A	131	73%	3.16
OZ	12	83	83%	1.82
WH	9A	143	83%	0.68
WK	10A	146	86%	1.55
WZ	13	86	100%	3.67
		AVERAGE:	87%	3.06
Meats				
LCQ	3A	125	75%	1.38
LHM	4	59	100%	1.97
LHQ	2A	122	83%	1.73
LHZ	6A	134	100%	1.76
LHN/PBN	9	74	92%	1.08
PBG	8A	140	100%	1.04
PBG	17	98	92%	1.08
PBN	1	50	100%	1.05
		AVERAGE:	93%	1.40
Metals				
CPN	18	101	91%	1.56
CPZ	8	71	89%	0.93
GOM	5	62	100%	0.58
GOZ	15	92	100%	1.33
		AVERAGE:	95%	1.10
Other				
CCV	1A	119	100%	1.93
CCZ	11	80	92%	0.92
CTN	16	95	100%	1.29
PWK	12A	152	83%	2.10
PWN	6	65	100%	1.35
		AVERAGE:	95%	1.52
	AVERAGE ALL TRADES:		91%	2.10

APPENDIX II
Seasonal Trade Calendar

(Trades Which Enter This Month, or Later)

	TRADE #	PAGE #
January		
CZ/WZ	2	53
CCU	1A	119
February		
SN/SX	3	56
LHM	4	59
GOM	5	62
PWN	6	65
LHN/PBN	9	74
March		
CZ	7	68
CPZ	8	71
LHQ	2A	122
LCQ	3A	125
SX/SN	4A	128
April		
SMZ/SMU	5A	131
May		
BOZ	10	77
CCZ	11	80
LHZ	6A	134
SX	7A	137
June		
OZ	12	83
July		
WZ	13	86
August		
SX	14	89
GOZ	15	92
PBG	8A	140
September		
WH	9A	143

	TRADE #	PAGE #
October		
CTN	16	95
WK	10A	146
CN	11A	149
November		
PBG	17	98
CPN	18	101
PWK	12A	152
December		
PBN	1	50

APPENDIX III
Index

<u>**PAGE #**</u>

APPENDIX IV
Bibliography

1. B. Graham, **The Intelligent Investor,** Harper & Row, New York, 1973.

2. R. J. Teweles, C. V. Harlow, and H. L. Stone, **The Commodity Futures Game,** McGraw-Hill, New York, 1974.

3. B. G. Gould, **Commodity Trading Manual,** Bruce Gould Publications, Seattle, Washington, 1976.

4. L. R. Williams and M. L. Noseworthy, **Sure Thing Commodity Trading,** Windsor Books, Brightwaters, New York, 1977.

5. J. Grushcow and C. Smith, **Profits Through Seasonal Trading,** J. Wiley & Sons, New York, 1980.

6. J. Bernstein, **MBH Seasonal Futures Charts,** MBH Commodity Advisors, Inc., Winnetka, Illinois, 1979.

7. P. J. Kaufman, **Commodity Trading Systems and Methods,** J. Wiley & Sons, New York, 1978.

8. A. Sklarew, **Techniques of a Professional Commodity Chart Analyst,** Commodity Research Bureau, Inc., New York, 1980.

9. J. Bernstein, **How to Profit From Seasonal Commodity Spreads,** J. Wiley & Sons, New York, 1983.

CPSIA information can be obtained
at www.ICGtesting.com
Printed in the USA
BVHW01*2230140518
516239BV00007B/75/P